TRAILBLAZERS
IN SCIENCE AND TECHNOLOGY

The Curie Family

EXPLORING RADIOACTIVITY

TRAILBLAZERS
IN SCIENCE AND TECHNOLOGY

The Curie Family

EXPLORING RADIOACTIVITY

Harry Henderson

CHELSEA HOUSE
An Infobase Learning Company

THE CURIE FAMILY: Exploring Radioactivity

Chelsea House
An imprint of Infobase Learning
132 West 31st Street
New York NY 10001

Library of Congress Cataloging-in-Publication Data

Henderson, Harry, 1951–
    The Curie family : exploring radioactivity / Harry Henderson.
      p. cm.—(Trailblazers in science and technology)
    Includes bibliographical references and index.
    ISBN 978–1–60413–675–3
    1. Curie family—Juvenile literature. 2. Curie, Marie, 1867–1934—Juvenile literature. 3. Curie, Pierre, 1859–1906—Juvenile literature. 4. Physicists—Poland—Biography—Juvenile literature. 5. Physicists—France—Biography—Juvenile literature. 6. Radioactivity—History—Juvenile literature. I. Title.
    QD22.C79H46 2012
    539.7'520922—dc23   2011011800

Text design by Erika K. Arroyo
Composition by Hermitage Publishing Services
Illustrations by Bobbi McCutcheon
Photo research by Suzanne M. Tibor
Cover printed by Yurchak Printing, Landisville, Pa.
Book printed and bound by Yurchak Printing, Landisville, Pa.
Date printed: April 2012
Printed in the United States of America

This book is printed on acid-free paper.

For my wife, Lisa. Her radiance has no half-life.

Contents

Preface

Trailblazers in Science and Technology is a multivolume set of biographies for young adults that profiles 10 individuals or small groups who were trailblazers in science—in other words, those who made discoveries that greatly broadened human knowledge and sometimes changed society or saved many lives. In addition to describing those discoveries and their effects, the books explore the qualities that made these people trailblazers, the personal relationships they formed, and the way those relationships interacted with their scientific work.

What does it take to be a trailblazer, in science or any other field of human endeavor?

First, a trailblazer must have imagination: the power to envision a path where others see only expanses of jungle, desert, or swamp. Helen Taussig, Alfred Blalock, and Vivien Thomas imagined an operation that could help children whose condition everyone else thought was hopeless. Louis and Mary Leakey looked at shards of bone embedded in the rocks of an African valley and pictured in them the story of humanity's birth.

Imagination alone will not blaze a trail, however. A trailblazer must also have determination and courage, the will to keep on trudging and swinging a metaphorical machete long after others fall by the wayside. Pierre and Marie Curie stirred their witch's cauldron for day after day in a dirty shed, melting down tons of rock to extract a tiny sample of a strange new element. The women astronomers who assisted Edward Pickering patiently counted and compared white spots on thousands of photographs in order to map the universe.

Because their vision is so different from that of others, trailblazers often are not popular. They may find themselves isolated even from those who are working toward the same goals, as Rosalind Franklin did in her research on DNA. Other researchers may brand them as outsiders and therefore ignore their work, as mathematicians did at first with Edward Lorenz's writings on chaos theory because Lorenz's background was in meteorology (weather science), a quite different scientific discipline. Society may regard them as eccentric or worse, as happened to electricity pioneer Nikola Tesla and, to a lesser extent, genome analyst and entrepreneur Craig Venter. This separateness sometimes freed and sometimes hindered these individuals' creative paths.

On the other hand, the relationships that trailblazers do form often sustain them and enrich their work. In addition to supplying emotional and intellectual support, compatible partners of whatever type can build on one another's ideas to achieve insights that neither would have been likely to develop alone. Two married couples described in this set, the Curies and the Leakeys, not only helped each other in their scientific efforts but inspired some of their children to continue on their path. Other partnerships, such as the one between Larry Page and Sergey Brin, the computer scientists-turned-entrepreneurs who founded the Internet giant Google, related strictly to business, but they were just as essential to the partners' success.

Even relationships that have an unhealthy side may prove to offer unexpected benefits. Pickering hired women such as Williamina Fleming to be his astronomical "computers" because he could pay them far less than he would have had to give men for the same work. Similarly, Alfred Blalock took advantage of Vivien Thomas's limited work choices as an African American to keep Thomas at his command in the surgical laboratory. At the same time, these instances of exploitation, so typical of the society of the times, gave the "exploited" opportunities that they would not otherwise have had. Thomas would not have contributed to lifesaving surgeries if he had remained a carpenter in Nashville, even though he might have earned more money than he did by working for Blalock. Fleming surely would never have discovered her talent for astronomy if Pickering had kept her as merely his "Scottish maid."

Competitors can form almost as close a relationship as cooperative partners, and like the irritating grain of sand in an oyster's shell that eventually yields a pearl, rivalries can inspire scientific trailblazers to heights of achievement that they might not have attained if they had worked unopposed. Tesla's competition with Thomas Edison to establish a grid of electrical power around U.S. cities stimulated as well as infuriated both men. Venter's announcement that he would produce a readout of humanity's genes sooner than the massive, government-funded Human Genome Project (HGP) pushed him, as well as his rival, HGP leader Francis Collins, to greater efforts. The French virologist Luc Montagnier was spurred to refine and prove his suspicions about the virus he thought was linked to AIDS because he knew that Robert Gallo, a similar researcher in another country, was close to publishing the same conclusions.

It is our hope that the biographies in the Trailblazers in Science and Technology set will inspire young people not only to discover and nurture the trailblazer within themselves but also to trust their imagination, even when it shows them a path that others say cannot exist, yet at the same time hold it to strict standards of proof. We hope they will form supportive relationships with others who share their vision, yet will also be willing to learn from those they compete with or even dislike. Above all, we hope they will feel the curiosity about the natural world and the determination to unravel its secrets that all trailblazers of science share.

Acknowledgments

I would like to thank Frank K. Darmstadt, executive editor, for his help and suggestions; Suzie Tibor for her hard work in researching and rounding up the photographs; and Bobbi McCutcheon for drawing the excellent line art. Additional thanks must go to all in the production department for copyediting, designing, laying out, and printing the book.

Introduction

Marie and Pierre Curie, their daughter, Irène Joliot-Curie, and Irène's husband, Frédéric Joliot-Curie, were one of science's most remarkable and influential family dynasties. *The Curie Family: Exploring Radioactivity,* one volume in the Trailblazers in Science and Technology set, illustrates how the Curies' painstaking research and startling discoveries were major factors in the development of nuclear physics. This new branch of science would have profound implications for our understanding of matter and energy and give rise to hopes for abundant power and to fears of ultimate destruction.

A TIME OF CHANGE

The world in which Marie and Pierre Curie grew up was in some respects already modern, but it believed in a future that seems rather naive from our vantage point in the early 21st century. A thoughtful European person living around 1890 would have looked back on a century of remarkable change, hoping that the next century would bring stability.

At the start of the 19th century, revolutionary ideas of liberty and human rights morphed into the imperial ambitions of Napoléon Bonaparte. By 1815, Napoléon had been defeated by a coalition led by Great Britain, Austria, Prussia, various German states, Russia, and other nations.

Napoléon (and the effort to defeat him) had, however, left important legacies in law, social institutions, and, particularly, the formation of the modern national state. Great Britain, already an industrial leader and colonial superpower, was gradually joined by a modern France (an important leader in the arts and sciences) and later by a unified German state (with growing industrial and scientific prowess, particularly in chemistry) and even a slowly modernizing Russia.

Socially, the desire for greater freedom and the need to address the plight of industrial workers led to attempts at revolution, notably in several countries in 1848 and in France in 1871. Nevertheless, reforms toward the end of the century (including the beginnings of a social insurance system in Germany) seemed to promise gradual improvement in living standards for nearly all Europeans.

SCIENTIFIC CERTAINTY?

Science and technology would play an increasingly important role in the expansion of these modern states. Steam brought a railroad and shipping network that could transport people and goods with unprecedented speed. The telegraph and later, the telephone, created a communications network that enabled governments and far-flung commercial enterprises to be administered effectively. The development of chemical engineering turned coal tars and other exotic materials into everything from cheap dyes to the first true wonder drug: aspirin.

Scientists, too, seemed to have cause to believe in a new era of stability and steadily advancing knowledge. Physicists had added to Newton's orderly theory of gravity an understanding of electromagnetism (the first "unified theory") that was expressed practically in electric generators, lighting, and motors. The basic properties of the chemical elements were increasingly well understood, as expressed in Dmitri Mendeleev's periodic table (for a modern version, see the appendix to this book). The rules governing chemical compounds and reactions also seemed to be shaping up nicely.

Although he may not have actually said that "Physics has come to an end," William Thomson, 1st Baron Kelvin, seemed to embody the attitude that by the early 1890s all the important discoveries in the physical sciences had been made. From then on, many scientists thought it would just be a matter of extending and applying them in more detail.

Only a few years later, that certainty, along with the idea of the solid atom, seemed to shatter. First, in 1895, Wilhelm Roentgen discovered X-rays, suggesting that there might be yet other kinds of electromagnetic radiation waiting to be found and used

X-rays could pass through solid matter. The next year, Henri Becquerel, experimenting with uranium compounds and photographic plates, discovered that uranium gave off a different form of mysterious, penetrating energy. Together with cathode rays and the beginnings of electronics, these discoveries revealed that atoms were not solid at all, but contained hidden particles and mysterious forces and energies. Physics had broken through to a new level.

A DOUBLE OUTSIDER

Marie Curie would seem to be an unlikely person to pioneer in the identification, extraction, and study of radioactive substances. She was not born in one of Europe's scientific and industrial centers, but in Warsaw, a city in Poland. At the time, as much as its people had a strong sense of national identity, Poland did not exist as a nation. It was occupied territory—in the case of Warsaw, it was part of the Russian Empire.

A young, talented Polish person like Marie Skłodowska who wanted to become a scientist or intellectual would have to go to a place such as Paris with an advanced university. But young Marie was an outsider in another way—as a woman, she had very little access to higher education at a time when most professions were viewed as exclusively male domains.

Chapter 1 of *The Curie Family* describes how a Polish family tried to provide a future for their daughters, Marie and her older sister Bronya. The Russian authorities tightly controlled formal education in an attempt to indoctrinate a generation of Poles into a foreign culture. Poles like the Skłodowskas did their best to counteract this propaganda program, creating a parallel, underground educational system, including even a floating university. Making a pact to help earn each other's tuition money, the two Skłodowska sisters were able to get an education at the Sorbonne in Paris, one of Europe's great universities.

In chapter 2, we find Marie beginning to shape her career as a scientist. She meets Pierre Curie, already a talented inventor and physicist. The two embark on what is at once a great love story and one of the most productive scientific partnerships of all time. Marie and Pierre are offered the opportunity to get in on the ground floor of nuclear physics, a science sparked by the newly discovered phenomena of X-rays and radioactivity.

In chapter 3, Marie and Pierre investigate the mysterious, intense radiation that persists even after uranium is extracted from an ore. Using instruments invented by Pierre and Marie's skill in chemical analysis, the Curies discover the source of the mysterious radiation—two new chemical elements that they name polonium and radium. Later they undertake a tedious (and dangerous) monthslong process in order to extract verifiable and usable quantities of the new substances. Their work is capped by a Nobel Prize in physics.

What should have been triumph became years of tragedy and struggle. As recounted in chapter 4, Pierre Curie is killed in a traffic accident, and a devastated Marie must struggle to resume her studies of radioactive phenomena. She is also embroiled in scandal and controversy involving both her scientific claims and her personal life. As she struggles with a growing list of health problems resulting from her extensive exposure to damaging radiation, the continuing value of her work is recognized by an unprecedented second Nobel Prize—this time in chemistry.

Chapter 5 describes the remainder of Marie Curie's career. In 1914, what Europeans had long feared became a reality—a devastating world war. Marie devoted her efforts to establishing a radiology service—including the use of mobile X-ray units. The result was thousands of lives saved and disabilities prevented. In the 1920s, Marie's attention turned back to her most cherished dream, the building and funding of a radium institute in memory of her husband.

By chapter 6, Marie has died after being increasingly crippled by the effects of radiation. Meanwhile, her daughter Irène had become a talented physicist in her own right. She met another young researcher, Frédéric Joliot, and another scientific love story and partnership began. As nuclear physics discovered new particles such as the neutron, continued to bombard atoms, and explored the possibility of nuclear fission, the Joliot-Curies discovered artificial radioactivity, earning them their own Nobel Prize. Later years bring World War II and efforts on behalf of the French resistance, Frédéric's role in designing France's first nuclear reactor, and his last years working in the face of cold war suspicions.

The conclusion describes efforts in recent years to celebrate and honor the work of the Curies and notes Marie Curie's lasting legacy in the growing number of highly talented woman scientists.

A final legacy of Marie Curie can perhaps be found in her fundamental attitude toward science, as expressed in her own words as quoted in her daughter Eve's biography of her:

> We should not allow it to be believed that all scientific progress can be reduced to mechanism. . . . Neither do I believe that the spirit of adventure runs any risk of disappearing in our world. If I see anything vital around me, it is precisely that spirit of adventure, which seems indestructible.

A Child of Poland

Marie Skłodowska was born on November 7, 1867, in an upstairs apartment of a girls' school in the old part of Warsaw in today's Poland. Marie's mother, Bronisława, ran the school. Marie's father, Władisław, taught mathematics and physics in nearby secondary schools. Marie had four sisters and a brother.

The family, while originally part of the Polish minor nobility, had lost their land in the preceding century. Marie's parents were well educated, cultured, and professional—but their lives were somewhat precarious, financially and otherwise.

Marie attracted the adults' attention at a young age. When she was only four, her older sister Bronya was stumbling through a reading lesson with their parents. Marie grabbed the book and read the first sentence aloud. There was silence . . . Marie assumed she must have done something terribly wrong. As noted in Eve Curie's book *Madame Curie,* the little girl stammered an apology. "Beg pardon! Pardon! I didn't do it on purpose. It's not my fault. It's not Bronya's fault. It's only because it was so easy!"

The silence had actually resulted from amazement: Somehow their youngest daughter had learned how to read without any lessons and could read better than her older sister! Nevertheless, they did not treat Marie as some sort of child prodigy. They wanted her to play and do other normal things for a girl her age, rather than burying herself in books.

AN OCCUPIED COUNTRY

Throughout Marie's childhood there was the always present reality that Poland, the country they loved and fiercely held on to, did not even exist on the map.

The land had been divided by three neighboring powers—Austria, Prussia, and Russia. The area containing the city of Warsaw was controlled by the

Marie Curie's birthplace in Warsaw (© *Hideo Kurihara/Alamy*)

The Skłodowski family in 1890 (left to right): Marie, father Władislaw, and sisters Bronya and Hela (*Musée Curie [Coll. ACJC]*)

Russian Empire under the autocratic rule of the czar. To try to prevent rebellion, the Russians sought to suppress the expression of Polish culture and ensure that children would grow up thinking of themselves as Russian.

One way to suppress a culture is to deny young people the opportunity to learn about it. Thus, in the government schools, children were taught the Russian language from a very young age. While children could learn Polish in private schools, these were closely watched by the government and were not allowed to give diplomas.

Poland had no realistic way of challenging Russia militarily. Instead, as Eve Curie pointed out in *Madame Curie:*

> The battle, therefore, had changed ground. Its heroes were no longer those warriors armed with scythes who charged the Cossacks and died saying . . . "What happiness to die for my country!" The new heroes were the intellectuals, the artists, priests, and schoolteachers—those upon whom the mind of the new generation depended.

An example of this sort of cultural guerrilla war can also be found in Eve Curie's book. One day, Marie, who had been promoted two years ahead of her age, was in class with her sister Hela. Their teacher was conducting an illegal class in Polish history. Suddenly, an electric bell sounded—two long rings, then two short rings. Both teacher and students knew what this meant. The Polish history books from which the teacher had been reading were spirited away to a nearby dormitory. The girls got out their needlework. When the government school inspector entered the room, he found the girls were dutifully knitting while their teacher read to them from a book of Russian fairy tales.

The official, a Mr. Hornberg, asked the teacher to call on a student to recite. Marie, the best student in the class, knew that she would be called, though she hated it. Mr. Hornberg asked her to recite the Lord's Prayer. Marie did so, in flawless Russian, as required. (It must have been quite a humiliation for a Polish Catholic to have to recite a Russian Orthodox version of the prayer.)

Marie was then asked to recite the list of all the czars of Russia and the names of all the current members of the imperial family. All of this, too, Marie did flawlessly. But as a final humiliation, she was asked, "Who rules over us?" Marie hesitated, and Mr. Hornberg repeated the question. Finally, Marie gave the only answer she could give: "His Majesty Alexander II, Czar of all the Russias."

After Mr. Hornberg finally left, Marie burst into tears and her teacher comforted her.

"POLAND IS NOT YET DEAD"

With the state schools so tightly controlled, many patriotic Polish families made great sacrifices to give their children an education in keeping with their culture. They believed that their children needed to have a strong sense of identity, so that their nation's independence might someday be won. This was certainly true of Marie's parents. Their attitude can be seen in the Polish national anthem used to this day, which begins:

Poland has not died yet
As long as we still live

After Marie was born, her mother had resigned from the school where she taught (and the family lived). The family moved to a high school for boys, and Władisław taught mathematics and physics. Unfortunately, he lost this position when the Russian official in charge of the school accused him of being a Polish nationalist. Each time Władisław obtained a job in the official school system, he was soon fired by the Russian bureaucrats. This oppressive atmosphere certainly had an effect on the Skłodowski children. In her book *Pierre Curie* (which also included autobiographical notes), Marie later recalled that:

Constantly held in suspicion and spied upon, the children knew that a single conversation in Polish, or an imprudent word, might seriously harm, not only themselves, but also their families.

The family struggled to make ends meet by taking in student boarders. There were tragedies: When Marie was eight, Zosia, her oldest sister, caught typhus from one of the boarders and died. Less than three years later, Bronisława died from tuberculosis—she was only 42. In her autobiographical notes, Marie would call this the "first great sorrow of my life," which "threw me into a profound depression."

The remainder of the family—Marie, her brother, Joseph, her sisters, Bronya and Hela, and their father, Władysław, faced an uncertain future. One way they kept their spirits up was to pursue intellectual activities. On Saturday night, Władisław read literary classics to the children. He also demonstrated principles of physics to them, using the laboratory equipment that he could no longer use in the Russian-controlled schools.

MARIE'S GRADUATION

Within the limitations of what Polish children were allowed to learn at school, Marie was an excellent student. Aided by her father's knowledge and enthusiasm, Marie mastered mathematics and physics, though she was handicapped by the fact that the Polish schools were no longer allowed to have laboratories.

When Marie graduated from high school in 1883 (at the age of only 15), she received a gold medal for academic excellence. The only thing that dimmed her pleasure was the fact that to receive it, she had to shake the hand of the top Russian education official.

After achievement came letdown—an episode of nervous collapse that doctors today would probably diagnose as depression. (Recurring depression would afflict Marie later in life as well.) Marie was sent to the country to recover, and the simple rhythms of country life (including dances and other festivities) seemed to do the trick.

In a letter to Kazia, a girl with whom she had become close friends (found in *Madame Curie*), Marie describes a dance festival called a *kulig:*

> I have been to a *kulig.* You can't imagine how delightful it is, especially when the clothes are beautiful and the boys are well dressed. My costume was very pretty . . . After this first *kulig* there was another, at which I had a marvelous time. There were a great many young men from Cracow, very handsome boys who danced so well! It is altogether exceptional to find such good dancers. At eight o'clock in the morning we danced the last dance—a white mazurka.

Upon her return home, Marie hoped that she could become a teacher in one of the free Polish schools. However, the family's financial situation had not improved, and she needed to find something that paid better. Her decision to leave was not an easy one for the 17-year-old Marie. As she would later note: "That going away remains one of the most vivid memories of my youth. My heart was heavy as I climbed into the railway car. . . . What experience was awaiting me?"

THE FLOATING UNIVERSITY

Opportunities for higher education were limited in Russian Poland. Marie's brother, Joseph, was able to enroll in the medical school at the University of Warsaw. But for women the only choice was to study at the Floating University, an underground—and illegal—school where the surreptitious classes were moved from place to place in an attempt to avoid the Russian police.

In her autobiographical notes, Marie captures the spirit of the Floating University:

> It was one of those groups of Polish youths who believed that the hope of their country lay in a great effort to develop the intellectual and moral strength of the nation. . . . we agreed among ourselves to give evening courses, each one teaching what he knew best.

Naturally such an informal school could not grant a degree. It also lacked the extensive, systematic teaching that a scientist needed, not to mention having no laboratories. Nevertheless Marie and her sister were exposed to liberal, freethinking ideas and some knowledge of the exciting developments in science and medicine that were coming from advanced countries such as Germany.

Writing in her autobiography 40 years later, Marie would have fond recollections of these days:

> I have a lively memory of that sympathetic atmosphere of social and intellectual comradeship. The means of action were poor and the results obtained could not be very considerable, and yet I persist in believing that the ideas that then guided us are the only ones which can lead to true social progress. We cannot build a better world without improving the individual.

TWO SISTERS MAKE A PACT

Marie and her older sister Bronya were close, and they decided that if they were to have a future they would need to take turns helping one another prepare. They agreed that Bronya would go to the medical school in Paris (one of the world's best). Marie would work to raise money for Bronya's tuition. After Bronya graduated, she would do the same for Marie.

At first, Marie worked as a private tutor. When that proved not to pay enough, she applied to become a governess. When she went to the employment agency, Marie listed her qualifications and experience. As recounted in *Madame Curie,* she had a perfect command of German, Russian, French, Polish, and English—she did admit her English was not quite as good as her other languages. She said that she could teach any of the standard school subjects.

Marie did receive and accept a job offer. She was placed in charge of the children of the Zorawski family, who owned a beet-sugar factory in the country north of Warsaw. The factory owner was a Polish nationalist. Besides teaching his children, he encouraged Marie to teach the children of the factory workers—peasants who had never had such an opportunity before. Such activities, if discovered, would certainly bring harsh retribution from the Russians.

Marie did get into some trouble, but in a different way. As described in *Madame Curie:*

> When the eldest son of M. and Mme. Z., Casimir, came back from Warsaw to Szczuki for his holidays, he found in the house a governess who could dance marvelously, row and skate; who was witty and had nice manners; who could make up verses as easily as she rode a horse or drive a carriage; who was different—how totally, mysteriously different!—from all the young ladies of his acquaintance.

For her part, Marie was almost as equally taken with the handsome, energetic Casimir, who was only a bit older than the (not quite 19) Marie.

Marie had gotten along very well with the Zorawski family. As the two young people spent an increasing amount of time together and fell in love, it seemed natural that when Casimir asked his parents for permission to marry Marie, there would be no objection raised. However, the elder Zorawskis, despite their affection for Marie, saw things differently. They believed their son could easily find a local girl from a wealthy family to marry, bringing greater status and perhaps business ties. Marie had no money and seemingly few prospects beyond caring for other peoples' children or teaching in a school. The marriage was out, although the two young people continued to be friends while Marie was in residence.

In *Madame Curie,* one finds that later, writing about her sister Hela (whose engagement had also been broken), Marie could vent some of her bitterness over her rejection:

> I can imagine how Hela's self-respect must have suffered. Truly, it gives one a good opinion of men! If they don't want to marry poor young girls, let them go to the devil! Nobody is asking them for anything. But why do they offend by troubling the peace of an innocent creature?

During these years of work Marie did her best to pursue her studies. Surprisingly, given her later career, it was not immediately obvious to Marie that she would become a scientist. As she recounted in *Pierre Curie:*

Literature interested me as much as sociology and science. Still, during these years of work, as I tried gradually to discover my true preferences, I finally turned toward mathematics and physics.

These solitary studies were encompassed with difficulty. The scientific education I had received at school was very incomplete—much inferior to the program for the baccalaureate in France. I tried to complete it in my own way, with the help of books got together by sheer chance. The method was not efficacious, but I acquired the habit of independent work and I learned a certain number of things which were useful to me later . . .

In one letter to her cousin Henrietta, Marie listed the books she was currently reading: 1) Daniel's *Physics,* of which I have finished the first volume; 2) Spencer's *Sociology,* in French; and 3) Paul Bers' *Lessons on Anatomy and Physiology,* in Russian. There are two remarkable things about this little list: the breadth of subjects (physics, social science, and medicine) and Marie's ability to work in several different languages: English (presumably), French, and Russian!

Marie eventually decided that chemistry was her main interest, so she arranged to take lessons from a chemist who worked in the sugar factory.

In 1889, Marie returned to Warsaw and her father's house. By then, her father had become director of a reform school and was making enough money not only to support himself but Bronya in Paris as well. Bronya in turn immediately told Marie not to send her any more money and told their father to send part of her allowance to Marie to begin to repay her. This funding, plus Marie's work as a tutor, meant that there would be enough money for Marie to go to Paris and begin her own formal studies.

STUDYING AT THE SORBONNE

The sight of Paris must have been amazing to Marie when she arrived. By the later part of the 19th century, the French capital had perhaps reached its height as a center of culture, the arts, and science. A series of universal expositions had showcased new technology (such as electric lighting). The Eiffel Tower, finished only about a year later, would become an icon of the new steel-ribbed architecture that would later rise as skyscrapers.

Upon enrolling in the Sorbonne, Polish Maria became Marie. As recounted in Eve Curie's biography:

. . . on her registration card she had written, in the French style, "Marie Skłodowska." But as her fellow students could not succeed in pronouncing the barbarous syllables of "Skłodowska," and the little Polish girl gave nobody the right to call her Marie, she kept a sort of mysterious anonymity. Often in the echoing galleries young men would encounter this shy and stubborn-faced girl with soft, light hair, who dressed with an austere and poverty-striken distinction, and would turn to each other in surprise, asking: "Who is it?" But the answer, if there was one, was vague. "It's a foreigner with an impossible name. She is always in the first row in the physics courses. Doesn't talk much."

At first, Marie lived with her sister Bronya (and her new husband), but Marie's father was concerned that involvement with the Polish exile community would get his daughter (and even the rest of the family) into political trouble back home. Thus, after a few months, Marie moved to the Latin Quarter, the area where many students and artists lived.

During her student years, Marie would live in several of the cheapest sort of apartments—eventually ending up in an attic of a private home, cramped but quiet to make it easier to study. She would have to climb about 100 steps to get to this perch, sometimes carrying a bucket of coal (when she could afford to heat her room). If there were no coal, she would go to a nearby library to study. (It was heated and stayed open to 10:00 P.M.)

Marie's diet was sparse, to say the least. Typically, she would have a cup of tea, or perhaps of chocolate, and a slice or two of bread. This would sometimes be supplemented by an egg or a bit of fruit. One time, after she had fainted, Marie was rescued by her alarmed brother-in-law. He and Bronya insisted that Marie stay with them for several days, and they fed her meat and potatoes.

The steps to the attic even found their way into one of Marie's poems, as quoted by Susan Quinn in *Marie Curie: A Life:*

Higher, higher, up she climbs
Past six floors she gasps and heaves
Students shelter near the sky
Up among the drafty eaves

Her poem continues on a more personal note:

Ideals flood this tiny room
They led her to this foreign land,

They urge her to pursue the truth
And seek the light that's close at hand.
It is the light she longs to find,
When she delights in learning more
Her world is learning; it defines
The destiny she's reaching for

For Marie, the academic courses were often as challenging as the living conditions. Despite the best efforts she had made to learn through informal classes and on her own, Marie lacked the systematic background in math and science that was expected of students at this level.

These handicaps make it all the more remarkable that Marie, after months of fierce devotion to study, finished her undergraduate degree in physics in 1893 first in her class. She then tackled the math degree. When she did not have enough money to finish the required courses, her French professors, recognizing her extraordinary ability, arranged for Marie to receive a scholarship set aside for outstanding Polish students. In 1894, Marie graduated in mathematics, finishing second in her class.

As she was finishing her math studies, an organization called the Society for the Encouragement of National Industry commissioned Marie to do her first real laboratory work—a study of the magnetic properties of various compositions of steel.

Science and Love

After the disappointment of being unable to marry Casimir, Marie had pretty much ignored social life and thoughts of romance. Besides, work took all her time, and her urge to master every aspect of science that interested her was very strong. However a new relationship gradually developed when she met an engineering student-turned-physicist named Pierre Curie.

PIERRE'S STORY

Pierre Curie was born on May 15, 1859, in Paris. His father, Eugène, a physician, was quite radical politically. In 1848, as revolutions swept through many European nations, Eugène had treated the wounded from the fighting that erupted in the streets. Later, he had supported the republicans who sought to replace the monarchy with a more democratic form of government and give the poor a chance at a decent life. When the republicans succeeded in taking over, they awarded Dr. Curie a medal. He would be equally bold in fighting a cholera epidemic from which many other doctors had fled.

The outgoing and active Dr. Curie nevertheless apparently saw something in his son that required a different approach. He decided that his son's sensitive and intense mind could not flourish in the regimented atmosphere of a public school. He and his wife, Sophie-Claire Depouilly, would take full charge of their son's education.

Pierre Curie (*top right*) with his brother, Jacques, and their parents (*Musée Curie [Coll. ACJC]*)

There was ample opportunity for young Pierre to learn science—biology, chemistry, and physics. By the time he was a teenager, Pierre had also shown considerable talent for mathematics, particularly geometry. However, Pierre's home education was not limited to science—he was also able to freely use his father's large library, where he could read in history, literature, philosophy, and other fields of the liberal arts.

The world in which Pierre grew up was not completely sheltered. In 1870 and 1871, his father again became involved as fighting broke out following France's humiliating defeat by the Prussian army. Rebels set up a provisional government, the Paris Commune. When it was suppressed by French troops, the Curie home became a makeshift hospital for treating the wounded.

A few years later, at the age of 16, Pierre entered university, and at 18 he earned the equivalent of a master's degree in physics. Not unlike Marie's family, Pierre's family was struggling financially. Instead of continuing on to a doctorate, Pierre had to get a job as a laboratory instructor. However, he and his older brother, Jacques, were able to pursue something that had fascinated them—magnetism.

MAGNETIC ATTRACTION

While magnetism certainly looked mysterious, by this time the behavior of ordinary magnetic materials such as iron had been well described by scientists. There was also the new theory of *electromagnetism,* which showed that an electric current could generate magnetic force and, in turn, a moving magnet could induce an electric current. By the end of the 19th century, this understanding was rapidly turning into what many called the age of electricity—electric lights and motors to run streetcars and even household appliances, powered by whirling dynamos.

The phenomenon that fascinated the Curie brothers was something stranger and subtler. They had discovered that if some kinds of crystals were compressed, they generated an electric current. This phenomenon is called the *piezoelectric effect* (from a Greek word meaning "to press"). A little while later, their mentor, Gabriel Lippmann (1845–1921), predicted mathematically that the reverse would also be true. Indeed, the Curies then confirmed experimentally that if one passes an electric current through one of those same crystals, the crystal became compressed.

The Curie brothers found a practical use for this knowledge. They designed the piezoelectric quartz electrometer, which can measure extremely faint electric currents. This device would prove to be very important for Marie and Pierre's later researches with radioactivity. (Pierre also developed a very sensitive balance scale, which would also prove to be useful when dealing with tiny amounts of material.)

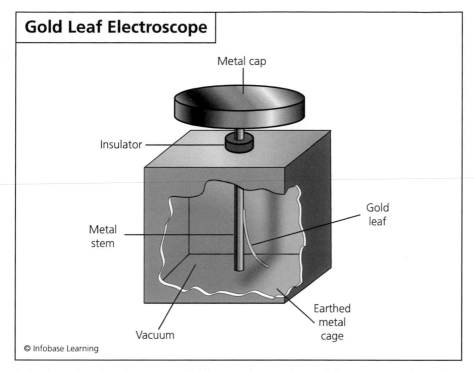

Gold Leaf Electroscope

Metal cap

Insulator

Gold leaf

Metal stem

Vacuum

Earthed metal cage

© Infobase Learning

A simple version of an electroscope, which responds to an electrical charge in proportion to its intensity.

Pierre made other important discoveries about magnetism. He learned that when some materials reach a specific temperature, their magnetic properties change dramatically. (This temperature is now called the *Curie point* in his honor.)

Pierre and Marie would find that their scientific strengths complemented each other. Pierre had more of a background in theoretical physics, enabling him to find explanations for newly discovered properties of *elements* such as radium. Marie's knowledge of chemistry and materials would lead her to emphasize the development of techniques for isolating and purifying the elusive radioactive elements.

Like Marie, Pierre would find that the merit of his work was often not enough to bring him the support of the French scientific establishment. In 1902, Pierre was rejected for membership in the French Academy of Sciences. The following year he was also rejected for a professorship in mineralogy. After Pierre's death in 1906, Marie would perpetuate his memory by

PIEZOELECTRICITY

Piezoelectricity might seem to be a rather esoteric subject, but the 20th century would find a number of important applications for this phenomenon. During World War I, faced with the need to detect deadly German U-boats, the French physicist Paul Langevin and his colleagues developed a form of sonar that used crystal transducers to pick up the returning signal. (This in turn allows determination of the distance to the submarine or other object that had been pinged.)

Piezoelectric quartz crystals also helped entertain millions of people through much of the 20th century. Ceramic crystal cartridges for record players were inexpensive and reliable, converting the movement of the phonograph needle to electrical current, which in turn could be turned into sound.

Meanwhile in the laboratory, the ultrasonic transducer enabled precise measurements of the viscosity (thickness) and elasticity of liquids and solids, enabling the analysis and creation of many new materials for use in industry.

Today, quartz crystals are used in a variety of electronic devices including watches and clocks, radio, television, and computer circuits. More humbly, they are found in ignition devices and lighters, where they can provide the needed spark without any use of fuel.

writing his biography and working to establish in his honor the kind of laboratory that she believed should have been provided for him.

FINDING A LAB—AND SOMETHING MORE

Marie now had to find a laboratory in which to work. When she asked a Polish physicist acquaintance if he knew where there might be some lab facilities, he suggested that his colleague might be able to help her. The colleague's name was Pierre Curie.

Pierre was well established in his field, having made several fundamental discoveries about the behavior of magnetism in various materials. He was also in charge of the laboratories of the Municipal School of Industrial Physics and Chemistry in Paris.

In her autobiography, Marie later recalled what Pierre looked like when they first met:

> He seemed to me very young, though he was at that time thirty-five years old. I was struck by the open expression of his face and by the slight suggestion of detachment in his whole attitude. His speech, rather slow and deliberate, his simplicity, and his smile, at once grave and youthful, inspired confidence.

Marie recalled that their conversation:

> ... soon became friendly. It first concerned certain scientific matters about which I was very glad to be able to ask his opinion. Then we discussed certain social and humanitarian subjects which interested us both. There was, between his conceptions and mine, despite the difference between our native countries, a surprising kinship, no doubt attributable to a certain likeness in the moral atmosphere in which we were both raised.

Pierre agreed to provide Marie with the small amount of lab space he had available. Pierre, about 10 years older than Marie, had lost his closest woman companion many years earlier. None of the women he had met since had shown much interest in science. In *Pierre Curie* Marie would write:

> [Pierre] had dedicated his life to his dream of science: he felt the need of a companion who could live his dream with him. He told me many times that the reason he had not married until he was thirty-six was because he did not believe in the possibility of a marriage that would meet this, his absolute necessity.

Marie returned to Poland for a vacation. Like many young Poles, she wanted to help her people develop and achieve their freedom. But science—and an anxious Pierre—soon beckoned her back to Paris.

BEGINNING LIFE TOGETHER

Marie and Pierre began to make their plans for the next few years. One thing was certain. As Marie later recalled in her autobiographical notes, "Our work drew us closer and closer, until we were both convinced that neither of us could find a better life companion."

Despite the impressive research Pierre had been doing and the recognition he had received for his groundbreaking papers on magnetism, he had never completed his doctorate. Marie was determined that even as she worked for her own doctorate, Pierre would finish his. Pierre, anxious for Marie to agree to marry him, set a firm date for defending this dissertation.

On the appointed day, Marie sat in the audience. As she recalled later in her biography of Pierre:

> I have a very vivid memory of how he sustained his thesis before the examiners. . . . I remember the simplicity and clarity of the exposition, the esteem indicated by the attitude of the professors. . . . I was greatly impressed: it seemed to me that the little room that day sheltered the exultation of human thought.

In March 1895, Pierre received his doctoral degree. It was followed by a promotion to a full professorship (along with a higher salary). Unfortunately, however, the available lab space remained inadequate for the Curies' work.

As much as she had come to love Pierre, Marie still hesitated to commit to their future together. Desperately, Pierre told Marie that if they married he would be willing to go to Poland and live with her there. Both of them knew, however, that the kind of science they wanted to do could only be done in one of the more advanced European countries such as France.

Finally, Marie accepted Pierre's marriage proposal without insisting that they go to Poland (they did agree to visit Poland). In July 1895, Pierre and Marie were married. Neither of them was religious, and they did not want an elaborate ceremony. No rings were exchanged. As Eve Curie notes in *Madame Curie,* Bronya's mother-in-law had offered to make Marie a wedding dress. Marie was less than enthusiastic. "If you are going to be kind enough to give me one, please let it be practical and dark, so that I can put it on afterwards to go to the laboratory."

After a party at Pierre's parents' home and a honeymoon spent riding a pair of new bicycles around the countryside, Marie was soon back in the laboratory to complete her industrial assignment. The Municipal School of Industrial Physics and Chemistry allowed her to use its facilities, but she had to scramble to obtain the steel samples she needed.

In 1897, when she completed the work and received her payment, she used part of the money to reimburse the Polish scholarship fund that had helped her with her doctorate. She saw this as part of her duty to keep alive the aspirations of the Polish people.

Pierre and Marie on their honeymoon (*Musée Curie [Coll. ACJC]*)

Even today life is not easy for professional couples where both partners have significant careers. In September 1897, a new factor entered into he equation: their first child, Irène, was born. (She was brought into the world by Pierre's physician father.)

SPARKING A NEW SCIENCE

By the middle of the 19th century, the basic laws of electricity were pretty well understood—at least as long as the electricity confined itself to wires, as in the telegraph and telephone. However, interesting things seemed to happen when high-voltage electricity was discharged as a spark into the air.

A German glassblower and technician named Heinrich Geissler (1814–79) took long glass tubes and pumped most of the air out of them. When an electrical spark was discharged into such a tube, the tube did not show the spark but rather lit up with a steady glow. The glow became known as *cathode rays* because it came from the cathode, or negative electrode, that introduced the electric discharge into the tube.

In 1879, William Crookes (1832–1919), an accomplished scientist, inventor, businessperson, and editor, wrote a paper about his experiments using a Geissler tube to generate cathode rays. Crookes then studied how the electricity discharges on a radiometer, a detector that uses a foil strip that moves in response to light or other electromagnetic radiation. He determined that cathode rays were not light but rather a stream of charged particles or projected *molecules*.

In 1896, the British physicist J. J. Thomson (1856–1940) carefully measured the charge and mass of the cathode particles. He determined that the particles had the same amount of charge and mass regardless of the material used in the cathode. It did not even turn out to matter whether the particles came from a glowing tube or Becquerel's newly discovered radioactivity in *uranium*. The Irish physicist George Fitzgerald (1851–1901) then coined the name the particles have today—*electron*.

In the 20th century, the vacuum tube and its electrical discharges would revolutionize technology, becoming an essential component of radio, television, and early computers. As for the electron, its discovery did indeed, as Crookes prophesied, "reveal to physical science a new world" within the atom and across the electromagnetic spectrum.

Marie was determined to be a good mother while still keeping her focus relentlessly on science. Following the death of her mother-in-law, Marie, Pierre, and Irène moved into a house with Pierre's father. An unexpected benefit of this arrangement was that Pierre's father could care for baby Irène while her parents worked. This would enable Marie to fulfill her obligations as a mother without giving up her precious scientific work.

SURPRISES FOR PHYSICS

With her family arrangements settled, Marie was free to pursue her own doctorate. This would be a breakthrough in itself—at the time, no woman had yet received a doctorate in science from a major university. Marie would need to pick a topic for her dissertation. Fortunately, the physics of the late 19th century offered a number of exciting topics, thanks to two recent discoveries.

By the 1890s, physicists seemed pretty sure they had a solid understanding of their field. Chemists were making rapid progress in understanding how molecules were formed from atoms. An *atom* (from a Greek word meaning "uncuttable") was believed to indeed be solid and featureless—as basic as one could get.

But while light could be absorbed or reflected by atoms, in December 1895 the German physicist Wilhelm Roentgen (1845-1923) discovered that an electronic vacuum tube (similar to that found in older TVs) could shoot out rays that could travel right through matter, provided it was not too dense. (For example, the rays could pass through the flesh of one's hand and outline the more solid bones within.) As proof, Roentgen published a photo of his wife's hand, visible in skeleton outline, ring and all.

What might this mean for physics? If atoms were so solid, how could these rays pass through them? In honor of their mysterious nature and the many unanswered questions, they became known as *X-rays*.

Only a few months later, in early 1896, a French physicist named Henri-Antoine Becquerel (1852–1908) was experimenting with some uranium compounds. He thought that the uranium could absorb sunlight and later *fluoresce*, or reemit the energy, which would form an impression on a photographic plate.

What he actually found was rather more remarkable. One day it was cloudy outside, and Becquerel, needing bright sun for the experiment, put the uranium sample and photographic plate away. Later, when he retrieved

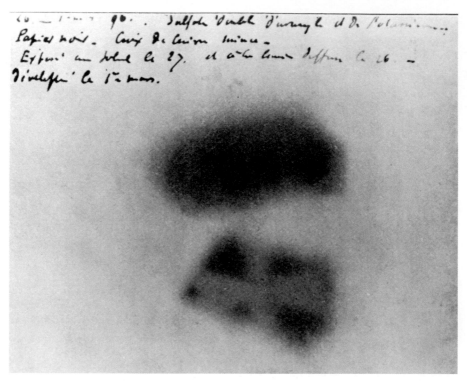

Becquerel's photo plate exposed by radioactivity, with his notes on the phenomenon   (*AIP Emilio Segrè Visual Archives, William G. Myers Collection*)

it, he was astonished to find that despite the lack of light, the plate had been exposed anyway, showing the silhouette of the uranium sample!

This phenomenon was even more mysterious than X-rays. Not only did the uranic rays pass through material like X-rays did, they required no tubes or electricity to generate. The uranium spontaneously produced them. But how could a solid atom do that?

Breakthroughs

Marie was especially intrigued by the uranium rays. She also realized that she had the chance to publish something that would not be just another in a long series of papers about an established phenomenon, but could be one of the first explorations into something new and exciting. That would be a good way to establish a career.

Marie's first laboratory was a musty storeroom full of assorted stuff, with barely enough room for her to set up her equipment. The most important piece of equipment was the *electrometer* that Pierre and his brother had invented. Rather than using a photographic plate like Becquerel did, with all the uncertainties of light and chemistry, the electrometer could make extremely precise measurements.

After days of painstaking practice to master its delicate settings, Marie could use this sensitive instrument to measure how the rays affected the ability of the air to conduct electricity, registering even tiny electrical currents. The total charge built up over time was proportional to the radioactivity of the substance being tested. Thus, while Marie was adjusting the electrometer with her right hand, her left hand was holding a stopwatch.

An important question was whether the strength of the uranium radiation depended on the uranium's physical state or chemical condition. Did it make a difference whether the uranium was solid or pulverized? No, not in the slightest. What about combining uranium with another element in a chemical compound? No, whatever kind of compound she prepared, Marie found that the only thing that mattered was a the amount of uranium in the sample.

Becquerel had already observed that uranium compounds that had a higher proportion of uranium emitted more intense rays. But Marie generalized this into a more fundamental hypothesis: The emission of rays in uranium must be the result of something inherent in the uranium atoms themselves, not in how they were arranged. In other words, the phenomenon that Marie named *radioactivity* is not a chemical property, but an atomic property.

Of course this discovery would result in many new questions. If atoms were not solid balls but had internal structure, what did that structure look like? One particle associated with atoms had been recently discovered—the electron—but were there others? Why were only certain kinds of atoms radioactive? Could it be because of something in their internal structure that allowed them to release what could be called atomic energy—or was it that the structure enables these atoms to trap energetic particles coming from space (including what became known as cosmic rays).

Marie and Pierre Curie used these instruments in their study of radioactive substances. The electroscope (*center*) and the ultrasensitive piezoelectric balance (*right*) were invented by Pierre. The third instrument (*left*) is an ionization chamber. (*Musée Curie [Coll. ACJC]*)

It would take a generation and more to answer these questions—and the next generation of Curies would play an important part. Meanwhile, as Marie began to test elements other than uranium for radioactivity, she discovered that the element thorium also produced Becquerel rays.

HIDDEN RADIANCE: POLONIUM AND RADIUM

Marie's first researches with uranium ores had revealed something perplexing. Two uranium ores, *pitchblende* and chalcolite, turned out to actually be much more radioactive than the equivalent amount of pure uranium. How could this be? Marie could only think of one explanation: There must be one or more as yet unknown radioactive substances hidden in these ores. Also intrigued, Pierre decided to join Marie in the quest to solve the mystery.

"Hidden" was a good word. Pitchblende, for example, is a mineral that contains many different substances and *compounds,* involving as many as 30 chemical elements. For each known substance, they would have to devise a chemical method by which it could be extracted and eliminated from the sample.

Material would have to be heated, sifted, treated with powerful acids, and otherwise separated out. Each resulting product, called a fraction, was then tested with the Curie electrometer to measure the amount of radiation it emitted. Logically, those fractions that were most radioactive should include the unknown radioactive element.

Working with a fraction containing mainly bismuth, the Curies found that after the uranium had been extracted the sample was much more radioactive than ordinary pitchblende or even pure uranium. Some unknown radioactive element must be present—something that had chemical properties similar to bismuth, since it had not been separated from the bismuth by the series of chemical processes they had used.

As they produced each successively larger and purer sample, Marie took it to a nearby colleague named Eugène Demarçay (1852–1904), an expert in spectroscopy. The *spectroscope* is one of the most important scientific instruments invented in the 19th century. It is based on the fact that each element produces a characteristic group of wavelengths of light (a spectrum). In the spectroscope, a prism breaks up the light and it is projected as a pattern of lines.

Demarçay dissolved the sample and painted the solution onto an electrode. Sending a spark through the electrode, a flash of light would appear,

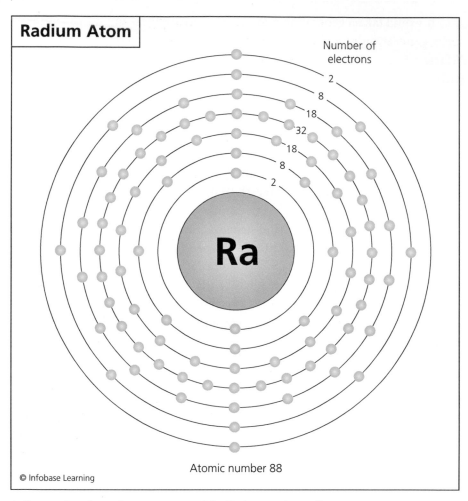

Radium Atom

Number of electrons

2
8
18
32
18
8
2

Ra

Atomic number 88

© Infobase Learning

A diagram that shows the arrangement of the 92 electrons in a radium atom

which had to be photographed by a precisely synchronized camera. Studying the resulting image, Demarçay looked for the spectral pattern (a series of lines). Finally one of Marie's samples was pure enough to yield sharp lines.

Demarçay knew the spectral patterns of all the known elements. He confirmed that this new pattern was one he had never seen. This meant that it must be a previously unknown element. Marie christened the newly discovered substance *polonium,* after her native land.

In July 1898, the Curies published this result. A little later, that December, they announced that another fraction, this one mostly barium, also had a hidden radioactive companion. They called this element *radium,* after the

Latin word for "ray." It was about 1 million times more radioactive than uranium, and it would make history.

MASS PRODUCTION

The claims of the Curies to have discovered new elements were literally based on the process of elimination. In a story from about this time, Sherlock Holmes is quoted as saying "Once you have eliminated the impossible, whatever remains, however improbable, must be the truth." If all that was left was bismuth or barium and those were not radioactive, some other element must be emitting the radiation they were detecting.

The logic seemed impeccable, but there is a saying in science that "extraordinary claims require extraordinary proof." Claiming not one but two new elements was extraordinary indeed. The Curies knew that they would have to produce enough of them so there would be no doubt that they physically existed.

This time, because the unknown radioactive substances were likely to be present only in very small quantities, Marie and Pierre would have to process a whole carload of ore to get enough polonium or radium to be definitive.

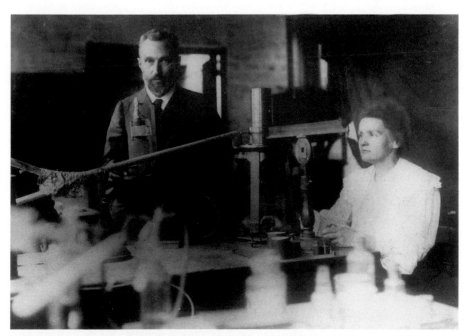

Pierre and Marie in the discovery shed (*Musée Curie [Coll. ACJC]*)

The old storeroom in the municipal school could not possibly hold what amounted to an industrial-scale ore-separation process. The Curies moved their operations to an abandoned shed in the school courtyard. It managed to be both drafty and poorly ventilated at the same time—hardly a good place to be using noxious chemicals.

While later accounts would portray what followed as a solitary effort, the Curies did receive some important assistance. The Austrian government, hoping they would find some use for the stuff, donated the first ton of pitchblende ore to the Curies. The French company that sold Pierre's electrometer and balance agreed to extract the fractions from the pitchblende that yielded the highest radioactivity. (In return they would receive a portion of the radium extracted and later turn the exotic element into a profitable business.)

Nevertheless the Curies faced a backbreaking task. In her autobiographical notes Marie recalls that:

> There was no question of obtaining the needed proper apparatus in common use by chemists. . . . Sometimes I had to spend a whole day mixing a boiling mass with a heavy iron rod nearly as large as myself. I would be broken by fatigue at day's end.

The cast-iron cauldron could hold about 20 kilograms (44 pounds) of pitchblende. The hut had no ventilation system. After heating the ore into a sludge and adding acids and other chemicals, Marie had to carry the whole thing out into the courtyard and finish the process in the open air, even though rain or snow might be falling.

Each cauldron of ore yielded a tiny amount of radium salts. It would take them more than three years to extract a pinch of radium . . . a tenth of a gram (.0035 ounces). They were unsuccessful at getting polonium—unknown to them, that element decayed too rapidly, with a *half-life* of only 138 days.

As exhausting as the effort had been, Marie later remarked in her autobiography that, "It was in this miserable old shed that we passed the best and happiest years of our life."

MARIE BECOMES A DOCTOR

In June 1903, Marie was ready to defend her doctoral dissertation. It was a historic occasion—the first time a woman had stood before the panel of Sorbonne professors to be examined for a doctoral degree. Marie calmly and systematically answered each question asked by the professor, sometimes

A 1904 illustration from *Le Petit Parisien* depicting Marie and Pierre Curie in their laboratory (*National Library of Medicine*)

drawing or writing on a blackboard. At the end, her old mentor, Professor Gabriel Lippmann, pronounced the verdict: Marie was awarded the title of doctor of physical science, with very high honors. Lippmann, by then a good friend, then added his personal congratulations.

The British nuclear physics pioneer Ernest Rutherford (1871–1937) happened to be in the area, intending to visit the Curies' lab. Although he had heard of Marie's examination too late to attend, he was invited to attend a dinner party organized by another close colleague, Paul Langevin, to celebrate Marie's degree. The bluff, outgoing Rutherford did not quite know what to make of the reserved Polish woman scientist. Eventually, however, their shared interest in atomic structure would bring a mutual regard and respect.

A RADIANT NEW INDUSTRY

In 1900, the world's first international congress of physicists was held in Paris. The Curies' work was a major topic of discussion. The glowing light from an object containing a bit of radium was dramatic. To the thoughtful scientist, the idea that atoms could generate energy spontaneously was even more intriguing.

The Curies, like many scientists of the time, had an attitude that might seem odd in today's era of corporate research and patent fights. The Curies did not patent the process of extracting radium. They believed their main focus should be on science and expanding human knowledge.

On the other hand, neither the Curies nor anyone else knew whether radium might find any profitable use at all. The substance was fiendishly difficult to extract, though admittedly a tiny bit could go a long way.

Pierre began to research the effect of radium on living tissue—he discovered (rather belatedly for their own health) that it could damage living cells. It then occurred that this offered a new way to fight cancer—one that is still a major form of treatment in some cases today.

By collaborating with the French industrialist Armet de Lisle, the Curies were able to set up the first actual factory to produce radium that could be provided to doctors for treatment and research. It was a fruitful collaboration: de Lisle had the advice of the world's experts on radium, and the Curies had the opportunity to secure a larger supply for their own research. However, what the Curies did not get out of all this was a significant source of income. The family's finances remained difficult. Pierre tried to get a better paying position, but despite his and Marie's achievements, the conservative French educational establishment looked down on the largely self-made scientist.

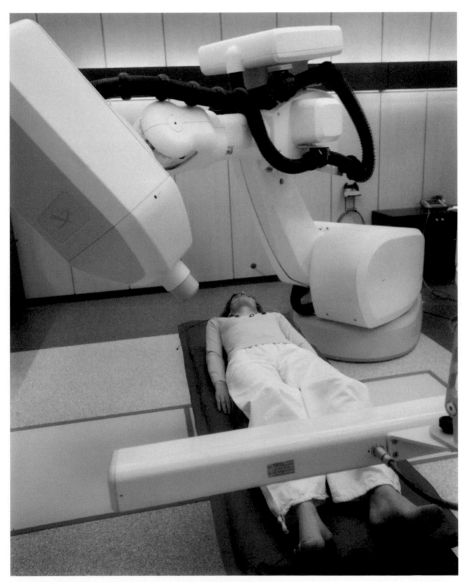

The CyberKnife® is a modern computer-controlled radiotherapy device. By using multiple beams, it concentrates radiation where it will do the most good, while sparing surrounding tissues as much as possible. *(Centre Oscar Lambret/Photo Researchers, Inc.)*

MODERN RADIATION THERAPY

The first attempts to use radiation to fight cancer were necessarily crude, although gradual improvement occurred, largely due to the efforts of Marie Curie to standardize the quality and potency of radium and other radioactive materials. Determining what dose (intensity and duration of radiation) is most effective against the tumor while minimizing damage to surrounding healthy tissue remains a prime consideration. Radiation therapy works mainly by damaging the DNA of cancer cells so they can no longer reproduce.

The radiation used in therapy can come either from radioisotope sources or (more commonly) from small *particle accelerators*. Modern radiation therapy units are precisely controlled by computers and include automatic safeguards against overexposure. Many radiation units use multiple beams of radiation that are focused so they meet at the tumor. This means that the highest dose of radiation will occur at the cancer site, while adjacent healthy areas will have received only the radiation in a single beam.

Treatments are often repeated over several weeks and calibrated to a dose that overwhelms the self-repair capability of cancer cells while allowing normal cells that have been damaged to repair themselves.

In a modern version of a treatment pioneered by doctors working with Marie Curie, small radioactive seeds can be surgically planted in a tumor, thus concentrating their effect.

Radiation therapy's effectiveness varies considerably with the type and extent of cancer. Radiation can be used to eradicate some tumors and shrink incurable ones, reducing pain and other symptoms and perhaps increasing survival. Radiation is also commonly used after surgery (as in breast cancer) to try to kill cancer cells that may have spread

An offer then came from the University of Geneva in Switzerland. Not only did they offer Pierre a good position and salary, they also offered to provide Marie with her own lab facilities. French nationalism then kicked in: Faced with the threat of losing their most "radiant" scientists, and at the urg-

beyond the surgical site. The development of modern medical imaging has also aided radiation therapy by making it easier to see the extent to which treatment has been successful.

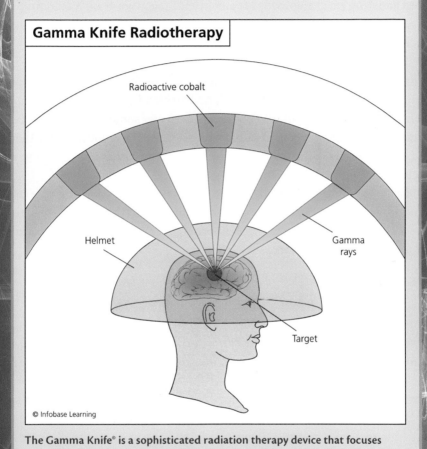

Gamma Knife Radiotherapy

Radioactive cobalt

Helmet

Gamma rays

Target

© Infobase Learning

The Gamma Knife® is a sophisticated radiation therapy device that focuses multiple beams of radiation on the tumor, maximizing therapeutic effect while minimizing damage to surrounding tissue.

ing of the distinguished French mathematician Henri Poincaré, the physics department at the Sorbonne came through. Pierre was offered the chair of physics in a program designed to teach medical students the basics of physics, chemistry, and natural history.

NEW TROUBLES

While their finances had improved, the Curies had a heavy workload. Pierre's position did not come with a lab, so the Curies kept working in the old shed. Also, when Pierre took his new position he still kept his old one, making for an exhausting teaching load. Meanwhile Marie, too, took a teaching position, becoming the first woman to lecture at France's most prestigious teacher training school at Sèvres, a suburb of Paris.

Health became an issue as well. Pierre began to suffer from severe bouts of pain and exhaustion. Marie, too, felt tired—she had lost nearly 20 pounds while working on her dissertation. The workload may have contributed to their health problems, but we now know there was something else involved—prolonged, sometimes severe radiation exposure. This could affect the skin and joints, suppress the immune system (making disease or infection more likely), and eventually cause cancer.

In 1902, more blows fell. Pierre, despite the prestige the Curies had brought to French science, was denied admission to the French Academy of Sciences. Marie also learned that her father, back in Poland, had died following a gallbladder operation.

SPEECHES AND STRUGGLES

As international excitement about the radium discoveries mounted, the Curies began to be invited to speak in other countries. In June 1903, they went to London at the invitation of the Royal Institution of Great Britain. The conservatism of the scientific establishment remained evident: Women were not considered appropriate lecturers. It was Pierre who had to speak for both Curies. Nevertheless, and despite suffering from sores on his fingers (due to a radium spill), Pierre explained the work to the distinguished audience, making it clear that his wife's contributions had been crucial at every step.

Back in Paris, the Curies received visitors. A welcome one was Bronya, Marie's sister. Bronya insisted that Marie get a new dress to celebrate her academic and scientific achievements. Characteristically, while Marie did choose a dress,—it was black, a practical color for not showing spills in the lab!

Health problems continued to plague both Curies, but Pierre in particular, who was now suffering from severe, chronic pain. Marie also experienced a miscarriage, an experience that was emotionally devastating. Writing to her sister, she told Bronya that, "I had grown so accustomed to the idea of

DEVELOPING A PICTURE OF THE ATOM

In the mid-19th century, physicists believed that atoms were indivisible. Chemists knew about many compounds (combinations of atoms), but the relationships between the various elements were not clear. During the 1860s, the Russian chemist Dmitri Mendeleev (1834–1907) had discovered that the elements could be grouped according to their chemical similarities to form what became known as the *periodic table* of the elements.

What was missing was a crucial link between physics and chemistry: What in the structure of atoms actually determined their chemical properties? Some depictions had the atoms looking like tiny balls with hooks and slots that could fit into each other to make compounds—rather like a Tinkertoy building set.

The first hint that atoms might not be solid and uniform came in 1879 when the British physicist William Crookes described how a stream of electrical particles could be produced using a high-voltage vacuum tube. This particle, called the *electron,* evidently was a part of the atom but could be stripped away under certain conditions.

The discovery of radioactivity by Henri Becquerel and the subsequent isolation of new radioactive elements by the Curies showed that other kinds of particles or energy could be emitted by atoms.

The New Zealand–born physicist Ernest Rutherford, his colleagues, and later researchers performed a series of experiments that revealed much more about the structure of atoms. The nucleus was found to consist of *protons* and neutrons and a variety of other particles have been discovered and grouped into various families by physicists.

the child that I am absolutely desperate and cannot be consoled." Bronya in turn then lost one of her own children to tuberculosis.

THE NOBEL PRIZE

At the time the Curies discovered radium the Nobel Prize was just getting started. The procedures for nominating scientists for the award were still being established. In fact, Marie Curie almost did not get the prize. In 1903, the French Academy of Sciences nominated Henri Becquerel and Pierre Curie for their work with uranium and other radioactive elements. Marie was not included.

One member of the nominating committee, the Swedish mathematician Magnus Goesta Mittag-Leffler, an advocate for women in science, wrote Pierre to tell him what had happened. Pierre was adamant—he wrote back saying that any Nobel Prize for research in radioactivity that did not include Marie Curie would be ludicrous. Apparently the prize committee reconsidered, and Marie (who had been nominated for the previous year's prize) was now included in the 1903 nominations.

In December 1903, Becquerel and the two Curies were awarded the Nobel Prize in physics. Interestingly, the citation for the Curies' work did not mention radium or polonium! At the time, these elements had not actually been isolated. This omission would have important consequences about a decade later.

A crowd of reporters arrived the very evening the award had been announced. The elder Curies were not at home—only daughter Irène and their nurse were there to answer the door. When the reporters asked, "Where are your parents?" six-year-old Irène confidently replied, "At the laboratory, of course." After all, that is where they were nearly always to be found! Irène then calmly resumed playing with the family cat.

Later, writing to a friend, Pierre complained that, "We have been pursued by journalists and photographers from all countries of the world; they have even gone so far as to report the conversation between my daughter and her nurse."

Because of their health problems and workload, the two Curies did not actually attend the ceremony in Stockholm, Sweden. Marie also continued to complain that the publicity caused by the award was flooding them with visitors and invitations to give lectures, making it virtually impossible for them to continue their work.

Finally, the uproar began to subside, and conditions began to return to something like normal. In December 1904, their second daughter, Eve, was born. There was one bit of unfinished business. A condition of the Nobel Prize was that the recipient gives a lecture, and finally, in June 1905, the Curies went to Stockholm. Again, it was expected that only men give lectures. Pierre gave the lecture but carefully explained how important Marie's part was in their collaboration.

In his Nobel lecture, Pierre, always in pain from his radium sores, warned that radium could be dangerous:

. . . in certain cases [the action of radium rays] could become dangerous. If one leaves a wooden box containing a small glass ampule with several centigrams of radium salt in one's pocket for a few hours, one will feel absolutely nothing. But fifteen days afterwards a redness will appear on the epidermis [skin] and then a sore which will be very difficult to heal. A more prolonged action could lead to paralysis and death. Radium must be transported in a thick box of lead.

It seems likely that Pierre was speaking from personal experience!

Pierre went on to say that radium and other recent discoveries might be quite dangerous as a potential weapon in the wrong hands. (After all, Alfred Nobel, who established the prize, had made his fortune from his invention of dynamite. And already millions of explosive shells were being stockpiled in the arsenals of the major European powers.)

Pierre asked, "If humanity can benefit by knowing the secrets of nature. . . . or if this knowledge will not be harmful to the world." Nevertheless, he closed on a more positive note: "I am one of those who believe with Nobel that mankind will derive more good than harm from the new discoveries."

The Nobel did bring some benefits to the Curies. The prize money certainly helped—they could now afford to hire a lab assistant. The Sorbonne agreed to offer Pierre a post that included a proper lab. In 1905, the French Academy of Sciences finally accepted Pierre for membership, though the latter wrote to a colleague that, "I have not yet discovered what is the use of the Academy." (Marie was not eligible for the Academy because only men were admitted.)

There was one line Marie refused to cross. As the value of radium for medicine and research grew, so did the monetary value of the substance. At one point, the radium that the Curies had already produced was worth more than a million francs—millions of dollars in modern terms. Marie refused to claim ownership of any radium—though through her institution she would control how it was parceled out to researchers.

SCIENTISTS AT A SÉANCE

One of the stranger incidents in the Curies' life occurred in 1905. It began with the Curies becoming introduced to a rather different circle of society— show business. An American dancer, Loie Fuller (1862–1928), performed at the Folies-Bergère in Paris. Her dances used what today would be known as special effects, including elaborate electric lighting.

One evening she brought her performance, lighting technicians and all, to the Curies' dining room and gave a command performance for the two Nobel laureates. Fuller wanted to pay tribute to the Curies, but she also had a question: Could radium be incorporated into her performances? She suggested that she might dance in a butterfly costume with wings glowing from luminous radium paint.

The Curies told her it would be too dangerous. She went ahead and used another kind of phosphorescent paint, but in one test the paint caught fire and an explosion singed her eyebrows. That was the end of that project.

However, Fuller had introduced the Curies to other celebrities, including the sculptor Auguste Rodin (1840–1917). Meanwhile, Pierre was reviving his interest in spiritualism, a topic that had engaged both Curie brothers in their youth.

Spiritualism (the belief in such things as psychic powers and communication with the dead) was a very popular topic in the late 19th century. While today mainstream scientists generally do not believe there is credible evidence for psychic phenomena, it is perhaps not surprising that a number of distinguished scientists of the time (including William Crookes, the discoverer of cathode rays) thought there might be something to it.

After all, X-rays seemed to magically penetrate skin and outline bones. Experimenters such as the Italian Guglielmo Marconi (1874–1937) were sending messages far across the sea using invisible electromagnetic waves. If atoms could mysteriously send out energy and if there was a whole spectrum of waves and rays that were invisible to the human eye, was it that hard to believe that there might be an invisible realm through which thoughts or even energy could pass?

On July 6, 1905, Pierre and Marie and several other reputable people sat around a table, holding hands in a circle. It was a spiritualist séance, conducted by Eusapia Palladino (1854–1918). Palladino, apparently an uneducated Italian peasant woman, had become internationally famous as a psychic medium. After appearing to go into a trance, Palladino appeared to levitate objects from the table . . . and then the table itself seemed to rise into the air! Other luminous objects floated high in the air.

Pierre tried to take a scientific attitude toward the proceedings. He carefully noted the initial positions of objects, the lighting, and other factors that might be involved in the performance. However, he did believe that some mysterious force was at work, some kind of energy that accumulated and then was discharged violently. While acknowledging that some sort of conjuring tricks might have been employed, Pierre and his friends believed they had taken great pains to restrict the medium's movements and to make anything she was doing visible.

Pierre concluded that Palladino was either a real medium or an extraordinarily skilled magician. (Later, in New York, two black-clad men who sneaked under the table during a séance observed Palladino raising the table with her feet. Palladino's career gradually faded.)

After these interludes and diversions, the Curies found themselves settling back into scientific work—but their remaining time together would not be long.

Difficult Years

Pierre had been suffering from stress and poor health, but by spring 1906 things appeared to be getting better for him. During Easter, he had enjoyed a visit in the country, taking special pleasure in watching his daughters (eight-year-old Irène and 14-month old Eve) play. Now, back in Paris, Pierre had rejoined the scientific world with some enthusiasm.

Pierre's intense focus made him somewhat of the absentminded professor. In *Madame Curie,* it is reported that one time Pierre had enjoyed a hearty dinner. The cook asked him whether he had enjoyed the steak he had just eaten. "Did I eat beefsteak? It's quite possible," Pierre mused. But distraction could have far worse consequences.

SUDDEN TRAGEDY

On April 19, 1906, Pierre, having spent the morning at work in his laboratory, unfurled his umbrella against the heavy rain and walked to a luncheon meeting where he discussed important issues. He then went back out in the rain to his publisher's office, where he was scheduled to review the proofs for a forthcoming publication.

It turned out the door to the building was locked because some workers had gone on strike. Perhaps disappointed, irritated—certainly distracted—Pierre dashed back across the street. He did not see the horse-drawn wagon coming, and the driver had no time to stop. Pierre was

Pierre Curie as a professor at the Sorbonne *(Musée Curie [Coll. ACJC])*

hurled to the ground and a wheel rolled over his head, crushing it and killing him instantly.

The police identified Professor Curie from the calling cards in his pocket. They contacted the dean at the Sorbonne. Together with the Curies' good friend, neighbor, and fellow physicist Jean Perrin (1870–1942), they went to the Curie home. Only Pierre's father was home, minding baby Irène as usual. As reported in *Madame Curie,* the elder Curie immediately guessed what had happened: "My son is dead. What was he dreaming of this time?"

When the news came to Marie, her reaction was a bit different. She could not believe it. "Pierre is dead? Dead? Absolutely dead?" In a daze, she contacted Pierre's brother and other family members and made the necessary arrangements. The death of one of the world's most eminent scientists brought international attention. Telegrams and letters poured in.

At the funeral home, according to the biographer Susan Quinn, Marie sat beside Pierre's coffin and felt a sense of communion:

> I put my head against [the coffin] . . . and I spoke to you. I told you that I loved you and that I had always loved you with all my heart . . . And it seemed to me that from this cold contact of my forehead with the casket something came to me, something like a calm and an intuition that I would have the courage to live. Was this an illusion or was there an accumulation of energy coming from you and condensing in the closed casket which came to me?

(Here can be seen an echo of the Curies' belief in spiritualism.)

CARRYING ON

Pierre's brother, Jacques, encouraged the grief-stricken Marie to return to work. Later, she would recall in her autobiographical notes that:

> Crushed by the blow, I did not feel able to face the future. I could not forget, however, what my husband used to say, that even deprived of him, I ought to continue my work.

As Rosalyn Plfaum recounts in *Grand Obsession,* Jacques maneuvered Marie, on a pretext, back into the laboratory. [He believed that] "her work would help her to survive. . . . It was too much for her. Nevertheless, like a rider mounting a horse which had just thrown him, Marie had taken the first steps back to a normal existence." The French government offered Marie and her family a state pension that could support them for life. However she could not imagine such a retirement.

On May 13, 1906, the Sorbonne stepped in with a better offer. She could have Pierre's academic post and could build the laboratory Pierre had finally been promised. Marie seemed hesitant about committing herself, perhaps because it would be a final acknowledgement that Pierre was no longer there. Writing in her journal (as quoted in Quinn's biography),

Marie again addressed Pierre as she wrestled with the possibilities of the future:

> I don't know if this is good or bad … Sometimes it seems to me that that's the way it will be easiest for me to live, other times it seems to me that I am crazy to undertake that. How many times have I said that if I didn't have you, I probably wouldn't work anymore? … You said that it was necessary that I continue no matter what.

Marie finally came to a resolution. She was determined to build a scientific institution that would both honor Pierre and acknowledge the importance of the work they had shared.

Marie's inaugural Sorbonne lecture attracted great attention, not just because of her work and her tragedy, but because Marie would be the university's first woman professor. In her lecture, she chose to look back at perhaps the most remarkable decade in the history of science, quoting her husband's words exactly:

> When one considers the progress that has been made in physics in the past 10 years, one is surprised at the advance that has taken place in our ideas concerning electricity and matter. …

Surprised indeed! First the electron, then the X-ray, and then radiation. Even as the Curies were working to isolate radioactive elements and their properties, physicists such as Ernest Rutherford in New Zealand were beginning to develop new pictures of the atom in which incredibly tiny particles interacted.

LORD KELVIN'S CHALLENGE

Just a few months after Pierre's death, the work of the Curies on radium would be called into question. William Thomson (1824–1907), now Lord Kelvin, was the aging giant of British physics. Besides being an important inventor (he had helped design the transatlantic telegraph cable system), he was a pioneer in the field of thermodynamics, the field of physics concerned with heat flow.

Kelvin had praised Pierre Curie's earlier work with magnetism. Thus, it was rather a shock to Marie when Kelvin wrote a letter to the London *Times* that suggested that what the Curies had called radium was not an element at all. Perhaps, he suggested, it was a compound of lead and helium. (Though this sort of compound might add up to the right weight, it was actually quite unlikely, given helium's extreme reluctance to combine chemically with other elements.) Kelvin's letter went on to suggest that the Curies should not have been given the Nobel Prize.

Marie, while furious at Kelvin's remarks, knew that many scientists would not be convinced the Curies had found new elements to add to the periodic table until they actually could isolate those elements in pure form. (The results of their earlier large-scale processing had been significant, but not completely pure.) Marie now undertook another painstaking series of processes that after several years had yielded a few silvery grains of radium metal.

As she worked, Marie wanted to learn all she could about radium. Making a careful measurement, she determined that radium's *atomic weight* (the average mass of its atoms) was 225.93 (where hydrogen, the lightest element, has a weight of 1.008).

Studying the radiation emitted by radium, she (along with the independent work by Rutherford and Frederick Soddy [1977–1956] at Cambridge) confirmed there were three types. One was the relatively heavy positively charged particles that Rutherford had previously identified, which would become known as *alpha particles* (or alpha rays). Another was beta rays, which were similar to the cathode rays that had been produced by Crookes

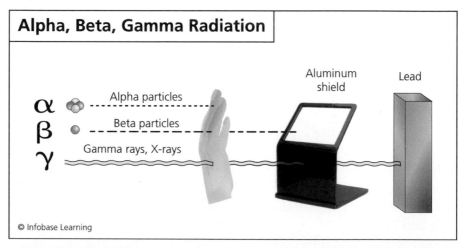

Alpha, Beta, Gamma Radiation

α Alpha particles
β Beta particles
γ Gamma rays, X-rays

Aluminum shield

Lead

© Infobase Learning

By 1900, three different types of radiation had been identified. Here, they are compared in terms of their penetrative power.

RADIOACTIVE DATING AND THE AGE OF THE EARTH

How old is Earth? At the start of the 19th century, even most educated people would have said "a few thousand years." However the development of modern geology early in the century revealed processes of mountain building and erosion that had taken millions of years.

By the end of the 19th century, geologists and physicists were in conflict. Geologists had refined their estimates to the hundreds of millions of years or more. However by 1897, William Thomson had calculated the amount of time it would have taken for the original molten Earth to cool, giving estimates ranging from only about 20 million to 40 million years old.

In their studies of radioactivity at McGill University in Montreal, Canada, Ernest Rutherford and Frederick Soddy had discovered that radioactive materials *decay* (break down) at a specific rate for each substance. They defined the half-life as the time it takes for half of a given sample of a substance to decay. They then suggested that using naturally occurring

(continues)

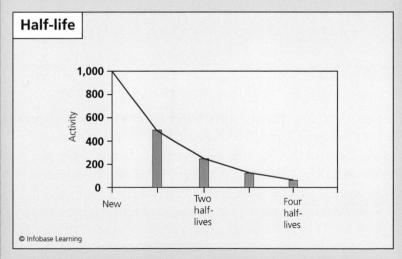

A graph that shows how the half-life of a radioactive substance affects its level of activity. Because each half-life cuts the intensity level in two, substances with short half-lives will lose most of their activity relatively quickly.

(continued)

radioactive elements such as uranium and thorium, which have particularly long half-lives, it would be possible to estimate the age of the Earth.

Rutherford tried out his technique by measuring the concentration of helium resulting from the decay of radium in a rock (the helium nucleus is the same as an alpha particle). He came up with 40 million years—rather high compared to what Thomson believed. When he announced this, Rutherford wrote (as quoted in a biography by Arthur Stewart Eve):

> I came into the room, which was half dark, and presently spotted Lord Kelvin in the audience and realized that I was in trouble as [my views on the age of the Earth] conflicted with his. To my relief, Kelvin fell fast asleep, but as I came to the important point, I saw the old bird sit up, open an eye, and cock a baleful glance at me! Then a sudden inspiration came, and I said 'Lord Kelvin had limited the age of the Earth, provided no new source was discovered. That prophetic utterance refers to what we are now discussing tonight, radium!' Behold the old boy beamed upon me.

Today Earth is known to be about 4.5 billion years old. *Radiometric dating* methods are used not only to determine the age of rocks but also fossils and archaeological artifacts. This tool has enabled a much more precise picture of the history of life on Earth, as well as of the development of ancient cultures.

(these were electrons). Finally, there was a type of energetic pure radiation similar to Roentgen's X-rays. These would be known as *gamma rays.*

Marie observed that the different types of radiation penetrated to different depths in different materials. Alpha particles were readily absorbed even by a thin piece of paper or after traveling just a few centimeters distance in air. *Beta particles* were more penetrating—about 100 times more so than alpha particles. They can damage tissue and cause cancer, although they can also be used to kill cancer cells. Finally, the gamma rays are the most intense form of radiation, penetrating deeply and capable of causing devastating damage to tissues. Together with Rutherford's work at about the same time, the Curies' research had created the fundamental understanding of radioactivity.

BUILDING AN INSTITUTE

The bulk of Marie's effort, however, was devoted to establishing the institute in honor of her husband. Her achievements and growing fame gave her access to the highest circles of science, and in 1907 Andrew Carnegie, the American steel magnate and philanthropist, agreed to donate $50,000 to establish a Curie Foundation that would fund scholarships and a laboratory. A favorable domestic political climate also helped raise support. The current French government was dominated by liberals who valued scientific progress.

The University of Paris and the Pasteur Foundation joined forces to create the Radium Institute. One part of the institute would be a laboratory for the study of radioactivity—Marie was given charge of this. The other part would be a medical research laboratory. (Given the important medical uses for radium, this arrangement seemed logical.)

Because of the demands of her new position, Marie had to give up her position training women teachers at Sèvres. However, she did not neglect her children. Marie decided it would be healthier for them if they lived in the country, so she moved the family to Sceaux, the town where Pierre had grown up, even though it meant that she would have to spend an additional hour each day commuting to Paris.

Like Pierre's father, Marie did not think the French public schools could adequately educate exceptional children. In *Pierre Curie* Marie would later write:

> In most schools, as they exist today, the time spent in various reading and writing exercises is too great, and the study required to be at home too much.

Perhaps in recognition of the extreme toll that a life as a dedicated scientist could take on the body, Marie also noted that, "Next to outdoor walks, I attach a great importance to gymnastics and sports."

Doing something about her children's education became urgent because Irène in particular showed every sign of scientific interest and talent. Marie joined her friends the Perrins and Paul Langevin, who all had children about the same age. They agreed to form a sort of cooperative private school that would give their children an excellent preparation in science and the arts.

Irène and the other children would have only one lesson a day, but the quality of the teaching would be very high—each day the teacher would be one of their parents or a colleague from the Sorbonne. The children would learn science of course—chemistry, physics, and mathematics. But they would also be exposed to art, literature, and history. For field trips they frequently visited museums or went to concerts.

Although this experimental school lasted only two years, Irène and Eve would flourish in it and be well prepared when they went on to other private schools. Irène made a firm decision to become a scientist and work in a laboratory like her mother. Eve, more outgoing, showed a greater interest in the arts and particularly music—she would become an excellent pianist.

The exciting world offered to young Irène and Eve would be marred only by the death of Pierre's father, their grandfather—their beloved "Grandpe." (Irène in particular had grown very close to him.)

VICTIM OF THE SCANDAL SHEETS

Marie had her first encounter with popular journalism following the discovery of radium. She quickly learned that many reporters knew little about science and seemed to always put the most sensational spin on any development. After the news of her Nobel Prize came out, the Curies were virtually deluged with journalists wanting photos and interviews.

It seemed unlikely that a battle over a seat on the French Academy of Sciences would mushroom into what today one would call a tabloid scandal. In late 1910, there was a single seat in the Academy open for a physicist. Marie was one candidate (the ban on women had finally been lifted). The other was Édouard Branly (1844–1940), a pioneer in early wireless telegraphy.

Branly was championed by many French nationalists and conservatives (primarily Catholics). This group was already disposed to be suspicious of Marie Curie, who was associated with liberal freethinkers. Some right-wingers in the press even spread the rumor that Marie was Jewish (she was not), appealing to the anti-Semitism that was prevalent in some parts of French society.

Liberal commentators rose to her defense, but on January 23, 1911, the Academy voted, and Branly defeated Curie by two votes. Marie kept her feelings to herself (at least in public) and plunged back into her scientific work. Meanwhile, however, she had another small triumph. Along with Rutherford and her good friend Jean Perrin, Marie had attended a meeting of the World Congress on Radiology and Electricity. At question was the need to establish a standard measurement for radiation—something vital both for research and for the preparation of therapeutic doses.

One proposal was that the standard unit be called the curie, just as other important units had been named for pioneer researchers. (For example, in electricity there was the volt and the watt, named for Alessandro Volta [1745–1827] and James Watt [1736–1819] respectively.)

Marie agreed, provided that a curie be defined as the amount of radioactivity produced by one gram of radium in one second. Marie was then assigned the task of producing the international standard radium sample. As described in her autobiography:

> [This] was a very delicate, operation, as the weight of the standard sample, quite small [21.99 milligrams of pure radium chloride] had to be determined with great precision. It was accepted by the Commission and deposited in the International Bureau of Weights and Measures at Sèvres, near Paris.

Marie would actively use this standard in later years. As she later wrote in her autobiography:

> In France the control of radium tubes, by the measurement of their radiation, takes place in my laboratory, where anyone may come to bring the radium to be tested.

A bit later Marie finished *Treatise on Radioactivity,* a monumental two-volume work. Opposite the title page was a photograph of Pierre Curie. The treatise was essentially a compendium of more than a decade's research on radioactivity. While publicly praising the work for its generous treatment of himself and other researchers outside of France, Rutherford privately remarked that the book uncritically rehashed much of his own work without logical order or critical commentary.

THE LANGEVIN AFFAIR

By spring 1910, Marie seemed to be showing a renewed interest in life. At one dinner party she was observed wearing not her usual dark dress or suit, but a white dress with a rose at her waist. Intensely private by nature, Marie had hinted only to her closest friends that she was "seeing someone."

Marie had always been a good colleague and friend to the eminent French physicist Paul Langevin, who had been a student of Pierre's. By 1911, Langevin was suffering in an unhappy marriage—his wife had little interest

Paul Langevin and Marie Curie with a group of women—rumors of an affair between Curie and Langevin created a stir in the popular press. *(Albert Harlinque/Roger Viollet/Getty Images)*

in science or education and complained that he neglected his children in favor of work.

It was perhaps not that surprising that Marie and Langevin would find science and love fit together, much as it had with Pierre. But Langevin was married. French society of the time had a complicated attitude about such matters. It was generally accepted that a married man could have a mistress, as long as he supported his wife financially and accompanied her on suitable occasions. It was as though a man could have two lives in two circles, as long as they were kept carefully apart. But Marie could never be a mistress in that sense—she was as fully independent and professional as Langevin was. The relationship between the two simply did not fit in any of the approved categories.

Autumn 1911 brought the Solvay Conference, the first of a series of international physics conferences sponsored by a Belgian industrialist. Marie was the only woman invited to the conference, which featured such luminaries as Albert Einstein, Ernest Rutherford, Henri Poincaré, . . . and Paul Langevin. There would be a lot to talk about at this meeting. Besides radioactivity, there were the latest studies of atomic structure and, at the other end of the scale, the new picture of the universe—relativity—developed by the great physicist Albert Einstein (1879–1955).

The popular press paid little attention to the momentous scientific theories. What aroused their intense interest was a group of letters (or perhaps

Besides Marie Curie, the first Solvay Physics Conference in Brussels in 1911 included such luminaries as Ernest Rutherford, Albert Einstein, Paul Langevin, and Max Planck. *(Science & Society Picture Library/Getty Images)*

copies of letters) that had passed between Marie and Langevin. While not explicit by modern standards, the letters made it rather clear that the two were romantically involved.

Rumors and innuendos flew. Again, it was said that Marie was Jewish and had wrecked the happy Christian home of the Langevins. Some stories even hinted that the affair between Marie and Langevin had begun while Pierre was still alive and that his tragic accident had actually been a suicide!

One lurid publication called *Excelsior* devoted most of its front page to Marie Curie. It included unflattering photos arranged like police mug shots, together with analysis of her handwriting and of the shape of her skull, purporting to find degenerate characteristics.

One of the milder stories, printed in *Le Journal,* tried for a more poetic approach:

> The fires of radium which beam so mysteriously . . . have just lit a fire in the heart of one of the scientists who studies their action so devotedly; and the wife and the children of this scientist are in tears . . .

Returning home from the conference in Belgium, Marie found that her front door was blocked by an angry mob. Marie and her daughters had to flee to the home of some Parisian friends. Around the same time Langevin, feeling angry and insulted by a particular journalist, challenged him to a duel, which fortunately proved to be bloodless.

For a while it looked like Marie might even lose her position at the Sorbonne, but her many friends and colleagues on the faculty rallied to her defense and secured her position.

A SECOND NOBEL PRIZE

Even as she was being tried in the popular press, Marie was being evaluated again by the Swedish committee that awards the Nobel Prize. Shortly after returning from Belgium, Marie received the news that she had been awarded a second Nobel—this time, in chemistry.

The first prize, for physics, had been shared by Becquerel (for his discovery of uranium radiation) and the Curies for their careful studies that had revealed that this kind of radiation came from something in the inner structure of the atom. This realization inspired physicists (particularly Rutherford) to begin to probe atoms by bombarding them with electrons and radioactive particles. This would reveal that atoms were mostly empty space—a tiny positively charged nucleus surrounded by a number of negatively charged electrons that corresponded to the element's position in the periodic table.

The physics prize was thus well justified by events. But over the decade that followed their initial discovery, the Curies had established the actual existence of radium and further analyzed its properties. Marie had also been instrumental in showing that the new element had important medical uses. (Although he had played an important part in the earlier work, the prize could not be given to Pierre because the Nobel is not awarded posthumously.) Quite logically, the committee decided that Marie deserved a new prize:

> for her services to the advancement of chemistry by the discovery of the elements radium and polonium, by the isolation of radium and the study of the nature and compounds of this remarkable element.

Marie's other life then rudely intruded. One member of the Nobel committee wrote to Marie and asked her not to come to Sweden to receive the award because of the scandal that had swirled around her. While whether she came or not would not affect her receiving the prize, Marie wrote back angrily:

> The Prize has been awarded for discovery of Radium and Polonium. I believe that there is no connection between my scientific work and the facts of private life . . . I cannot accept the idea in principle that the appreciation of the value of scientific work should be influenced by libel and slander concerning private life.

Under the stress of the scandal and the prize, Marie lost weight and was not feeling well. Nevertheless she, together with her sister Bronya and her daughter Irène, did make the trip to Sweden, where the prize was awarded on December 10, 1911.

Marie, wearing a simple black lace dress, stood before the rostrum to deliver her Nobel address. She was the first woman ever to do so. (She had not traveled to Sweden for her first Nobel in 1903.) Graciously and carefully she explained the context of her work with radium and polonium, giving due credit to other researchers—particularly Ernest Rutherford, who had received his own Nobel Prize in 1908. At the same time she proudly explained how her work had done so much to establish a new kind of physics.

In her Nobel lecture Marie, looking back, pointed out that:

. . . now, only 15 years after Becquerel's discovery, we are face to face with a whole world of new phenomena belonging to a field which, despite its close connexion with the fields of physics and chemistry, is particularly well-

ERNEST RUTHERFORD: ATOMIC EXPLORER

Ernest Rutherford (1871–1937) came from the other side of the world from Marie Curie. He grew up in New Zealand, the son of a farmer, skilled in all things mechanical. His growing interest in science led Rutherford to a degree in mathematics and physics at Canterbury College in Christchurch, New Zealand. There he studied radio waves—a new phenomenon at the time, as well as other aspects of electromagnetism.

A desire for better scientific facilities and opportunities led Rutherford to accept a scholarship to Cambridge University in England where he went to work at the Cavendish, England's premier physics laboratory.

The discovery of X-rays by Roentgen in 1895 inspired Rutherford to use this energetic form of radiation to explore the structure and behavior of atoms. Studying *ionization* (the acquiring of electric charge) by atoms in a gas, Rutherford used his mechanical skills to build delicate instruments.

By 1898, Rutherford had turned his attention to the uranium radiation that Becquerel had discovered in 1896 and that the Curies were already studying in detail. Observing the effects of uranium rays, Rutherford distinguished the heavier alpha particles from the much smaller beta particles (or rays). He also discovered that all radioactive elements decay at uniform rates and measured the half-lives of many substances.

Rutherford's greatest triumph came in 1919, when he discovered that when nitrogen gas was bombarded with alpha particles, some hydrogen appeared. Rutherford recognized the hydrogen as actually being a positively charged particle that had been knocked out of the nucleus of the nitrogen atom. He suggested that this particle be called the proton, from a Greek word meaning "first one." The next year Rutherford also suggested the possible existence of an uncharged nuclear particle, the neutron. (It was confirmed in 1932 by Chadwick.)

Rutherford and Marie Curie were rivals, sometimes coming up with different versions of the same discovery or theory. But the two rivals also became good friends.

defined. In this field the importance of radium from the viewpoint of general theories has been decisive.

Marie went on to note that researchers had by that time identified about 30 new radioactive substances—either new elements or radioactive *isotopes* of known elements. In doing so scientists were now working with incredibly tiny amounts of substances, engaging it what Marie called "the chemistry of the imponderable."

Winning one Nobel Prize is remarkable. Winning two, and in different fields at that, is extraordinary. Other than Marie Curie, among individual recipients, only Linus Pauling shares this distinction, winning the chemistry prize in 1954 and the peace prize in 1962.

RECUPERATION

Despite this new Nobel triumph, Marie returned home from Sweden in poor health, physically and mentally. The stress brought about by the Langevin controversy and constant hounding by the press triggered one of the severe depressions that plagued her all her life.

Marie was also suffering from a severe kidney problem. She was running a high fever, and her doctors thought she was too weak to survive an operation. She lay in a private clinic under an assumed name, with no visitors allowed. Nevertheless, the secrecy only attracted rumors—one of which was that Marie was actually in the maternity ward, about to give birth to Langevin's child. This was refuted by Marie agreeing to release her medical records, which indeed indicated a kidney infection.

After Marie had recovered enough to be moved, Bronya rented a house for them (using their maiden name, Skłodowska). In March 1911, Marie was able to return to her regular apartment in the city, where she met to discuss continuing issues involving the radium standard. (Another physicist had prepared what he claimed to be a more accurate sample, but tests proved that Marie's was superior.)

Finally, the doctors decided that Marie could have the necessary kidney surgery. The effects on her still weak body were severe. The pain was excruciating and her weight, already only 123 pounds (56 kg), dropped to 103 pounds (47 kg). Fearing that she was dying, Marie anxiously conferred with a friend, Georges Gouy, asking him to help her make arrangements for her daughters' continuing education, the work of the Radium Institute, and the proper allocation of the radium under her control. While Georges believed that Marie would recover (and told her so), he agreed that he would carry out her wishes if necessary.

As Marie finally began to recover, she was visited by a delegation of academics led by Henryk Sienkewicz (1846–1916), who had won the Nobel Prize in literature for his novel *Quo Vadis*. They urged Marie to return to Poland, where the Scientific Society of Warsaw offered to build her a Radium Institute. Their plea appealed to her as a Polish patriot, as quoted in *Madame Curie:*

> We are losing confidence in our intellectual faculties. We are being lowered in the opinion of our enemies, and we are abandoning hope for the future. . . . Possessing you in Warsaw we should feel stronger, we should lift our heads now bent under so many misfortunes. May our prayers be granted. Do not repulse our hands which are stretched out to you.

This heartfelt plea no doubt moved Marie, but her commitment to the Radium Institute in Paris being built in her husband's memory, as well as concern for the educational and career prospects for her daughters, made her decide against the proposal. However, she offered to send two of her talented Polish assistants to Warsaw to supervise the establishment of the institute there, and she offered to provide advice as needed. This proposal was accepted by all concerned.

Marie then went to a health spa in Thonon-les-Bains near the French Alps. Ever the scientist, she recorded every aspect of her health daily, including temperature, fluid intake, intensity and duration of pain, and even the appearance of her urine.

During this time, Marie took comfort by exchanging letters with daughter Irène, now 14. The letters, addressed via a third party to conceal their identity, recounted events such as Irène's teaching little sister Eve to ride a bicycle, as well as her questions about science and world affairs.

ENGLAND AND THE SUFFRAGISTS

After further recovery, Marie traveled to England with her two daughters (using her maiden name, Skłodowska) and stayed with a good friend and colleague Hertrha Ayrton (1854–1923), who was also a physicist and a widow. Their conversations included the topic of women's suffrage (gaining women the right to vote).

Earlier, Hertha had sent Marie a petition to sign on behalf of a group of suffragists. In her letter (printed in Denis Brian's *The Curies*), she explained:

I am a member of the association whose leaders are now in prison, and I know those leaders personally and look on them as persons of the utmost nobility of mind and greatness of purpose.

Marie had signed the petition, saying that she:

was very touched by the struggle of English women for their rights. I admire them very much and I wish for their success. . . . I accept your using my name for the petition because I have great confidence in your judgment and I am convinced that your sympathy must be justified.

With indifference to their demands being met by growing militancy, it would be almost another decade before women won the right to vote in England and the United States.

A VISIT WITH EINSTEIN

In spring 1913, Marie was back teaching at the Sorbonne. When she heard that Einstein was visiting the city to address the French Society of Physics, she invited the famous physicist and his wife to stay. They enjoyed one another's company so much that they agreed to meet later in Zürich and hike in the Swiss Alps together.

The notoriously absentminded Einstein amused the Curie girls, particularly Eve, according to biographer Rosalyn Pfaum:

[Eve] was amused at the way Einstein circulated absentmindedly among the boulders, so deep in conversation that he walked alongside deep crevasses and toiled up the steep rocks without noticing them.

The other side of Einstein's absentmindedness was his remarkable intuition. On that same trip, Einstein suddenly seized Marie's arm, exclaiming to her, "You understand, what I need to know is exactly what happens to the passengers in an elevator when it falls into emptiness." This image reflects the ability to shift frames of reference in order to understand the relationship of mass, velocity, and space—the elements of relativity.

Indeed, besides being good friends, the two physicists had much to talk about scientifically. Essentially physics had split into two quite distinct fields dealing with the very large (relativity) and the very small (nuclear physics).

Einstein was quite interested in what Curie and others had been finding out about radioactivity.

While the phenomenon had been carefully observed, no one yet knew what made some atoms unstable. There was also growing speculation that a way might someday be found to deliberately trigger the release of huge amounts of energy from the atom. (In 1914, the British writer H. G. Wells would publish a story, "The World Set Free," in which scientists develop an immensely powerful atomic explosive such that "a man could carry about in a handbag an amount of latent energy sufficient to wreck half a city.")

In fall 1912, Marie returned to Paris, found the apartment where she would live the rest of her life, and finally, in December, returned to the lab. The legal separation of the Langevins had been completed without further implicating Marie. She and Paul would remain friends, but she would have no more affairs with him or anyone else.

Marie's life now belonged to her work—in particular the establishment and operation of the Radium Institute, which opened its doors in August 1914. That same month Europe erupted in war, and Marie would face a new kind of challenge.

A Life of Service

With the call-up of nearly all able-bodied men to war, the work of the Radium Institute would have to be postponed. Looking at her native land, there was little she could do—Poland had been caught in the middle (as usual) when Russia and Britain and France faced off against Austria-Hungary and Germany. With communications disrupted, Marie lost contact with her Polish relatives. Meanwhile, Paris was likely to be the target of a German invasion, so Marie left her children in the coastal village in Brittany where they had been spending the summer.

Marie felt great loyalty to France, her adopted country. Writing to Paul Langevin at the beginning of 1915, Marie made it clear that she was "resolved to put all my strength at the service of my adopted country, since I cannot do anything for my unfortunate native country right now."

By September 2, 1914, citizens of Paris could see the flashes of German artillery on the horizon. The French government evacuated south to Bordeaux. The government requested that Marie join them there. As she rode in the train car with government officials, she took along in a lead box France's entire supply of radium for research—a single gram.

After the radium was safely deposited in Bordeaux, Marie took a train back to Paris. Marie wrote to her daughter Irène, warning her that they might soon be cut off as Paris came under siege:

If that should happen, [you should] endure it with courage, for our personal desires are nothing compared to the great struggle that is now under way. You must feel responsible for your sister and take care of her if we should be separated for a longer time than I expected.

As the German army led by General Alexander von Kluck neared the city, he halted the advance and sent his army to sweep southeast around the city in a bid to surround and destroy or capture the retreating French troops. If he had succeeded, France could have been dealt a blow from which it could not recover and the outcome of World War I might have been quite different.

Fortunately, French resourcefulness (5,000 reinforcements were rushed up using every means available, including Parisian taxis) and the approaching British army combined to halt the German advance and push the enemy forces away from the city. Paris was saved.

There was thus no siege, and Marie and Irène were able to stay in communication by letter. Life was getting difficult for the 16 year-old-girl. Because of their Polish accents, some of the villagers regarded the Curie children with suspicion. As Irène wrote to her mother:

> they say I'm a German spy, and that when I go out with a little dish to collect blackberries that I'm bringing food in the pail to a hidden German spy. They also say that I'm a German man dressed as a woman, etc.

Marie could not spend much time worrying about her daughters' problems. She had realized that there was a vital service she could offer her country as it faced a war of unprecedented destructiveness. That other physics surprise of the 1890s, Roentgen's X-rays, could be put to good use.

LIFESAVING X-RAYS

By this time, doctors had been using X-rays for a number of years. With their aid, the exact location and extent of an injury such as a broken or fractured bone could be pinpointed and wounds could be examined for bullets or pieces of shrapnel.

Fast, effective treatment for extraction of bullets or setting of bones could mean a greater chance of survival and less pain for the injured. The war had brought a great increase in the effectiveness of artillery and other weapons and that meant more people could be injured in a single battle than had been hurt in entire previous wars. Battlefield medicine was still rudimentary, and hardworking doctors were frequently overwhelmed. By allowing for faster treatment, X-rays could also help cope with the workload of medical personnel.

As much as X-rays could help the military, there was a major problem. X-ray equipment was bulky and normally only found in hospitals or a few doctors' offices, not in the tents of military field hospitals. It could take many days to transport a wounded soldier to a place where there was an X-ray machine. But Marie devised a plan: She would bring the X-ray machines closer to the battlefield.

Aided by her prestige, Marie convinced the government to set up military *radiology* centers. Scrounging every bit of X-ray equipment she could find, the centers began to save limbs and lives.

THE "LITTLE CURIES"

However, only a limited number of such centers could be built. Marie needed a more flexible way to bring X-ray facilities to where they were needed as the battlefront shifted. She decided to create the first mobile X-ray units. As newly appointed director of the Red Cross Radiology Service, Marie was able to get financial donations. Some wealthy supporters even donated their cars.

Marie then designed her prototype mobile X-ray unit, which she describes in her biographical notes:

> I fitted up, with the help of the Red Cross, a radiologic car. It was simply a touring motorcar, arranged for the transport of a complete radiologic apparatus, together with a dynamo [generator] that was worked by the engine of the car, and furnished the electric current necessary for the production of the rays. This car could come at the call of any of the hospitals, large or small, in the surroundings of Paris. Cases of urgent need were frequent, for these hospitals had to take care of the wounded who could not be transported to more distant places.

Marie decided that she wanted to learn how to operate a mobile X-ray unit herself. First she had to learn to drive a car and learn how to repair it if it broke down. She also studied anatomy and the operation of the X-ray equipment so she could take proper images. As she trained herself, Marie also trained her first assistant—her daughter Irène, who was now 17 years old.

By October 1914, the first 20 radiology vans were ready for service. The soldiers began to call these welcome visitors "petites Curies," little Curies. In

Marie in a "Petite Curie"—these X-ray vans saved many wounded soldiers in World War I. *(Musée Curie [Coll. ACJC])*

the biography by Susan Quinn, Marie describes a bit of what it felt like to do this work:

> [Examining patients] lasts as long as is necessary, time is forgotten, all that matters is getting the job done with care. Sometimes, a difficult case slows things down, other times, the work proceeds rapidly. Finally the task is finished. The team packs the equipment in the cases and returns to its base, to begin again the same day or else the next.

In his biography of Marie Curie, Robert Reid quotes harrowing details from records made by Marie and Irène in the field:

> Bullet in the forearm . . . Numerous shell splinters and fracture . . . Ball shrapnel in right hand . . . rifle bullet in left buttock. Depth of wound 10.9 cm. Examination of cranium. Rifle bullet in central region viewed in profile.

The clinical descriptions perhaps protected the Curies from the full emotional impact at the time, but Marie later wrote in her autobiography that:

MEDICAL IMAGING

The X-ray provided the first means to peer into the body without cutting it open. Today, ordinary X-rays are still widely used: for example, a quick chest X-ray is often ordered by a doctor who suspects his or her patient may have pneumonia or another lung problem. Now, however, the image is likely to be captured by a sensor (rather like that in a digital camera) rather than a piece of film.

Sometimes it is necessary to see how structures within the body move and interact with one another. Fluoroscopy uses a screen that is coated with a fluorescent substance that creates a glowing image. The image from the X-rays is amplified and viewed through a television system, giving a real-time view of what is going on inside the body. Sometimes special materials called contrasts are swallowed by or injected into the patient. They help outline and sharpen the structures. Blood flow and digestion can be studied and obstructions identified. Some contrasts use radioisotopes.

The development of computers has revolutionized imaging by allowing precise control of the radiation being sent into the body and the depiction of the resulting image. The computed tomography (CT or Cat scan) uses a rotating X-ray generator to make as many as 64 or more separate cross-sectional images that can be assembled by computer software into a highly detailed 3D image of organs and other structures. The speed and accuracy of CT make it particularly useful in diagnosing a life-threatening condition such as a brain hemorrhage.

Two other imaging techniques have the advantage of not exposing the patient to radiation. Ultrasound uses high-frequency sound waves to provide a real-time image of soft tissue structures (including a fetus in the mother's womb). MRI (magnetic resonance imaging) uses a powerful magnetic field that temporarily distorts the orientation of nuclei in atoms in the body. When the nuclei spring back, they emit radio signals that can be used to build up a detailed image of body structures.

Doctors today thus have a variety of powerful tools that they can choose from according to what they are looking for.

Marie Curie wearing one of her ubiquitous black dresses—but looking radiant in a dignified sort of way (*Library of Congress*)

To hate the very idea of war, it ought to be sufficient to see once what I have seen so many times, over those years, men and boys brought to the advanced ambulance in a mixture of mud and blood, many of them dying of their injuries and many others recovering but slowly, in the space of months, with pain and suffering.

In later years, Marie would support peace efforts, but she was not an absolute pacifist. She believed that France must protect her interests in any negotiations.

Mother and daughter spent months driving their van and taking X-rays. (Irène would later receive a medal for her service.) As with the work with radium, there would be a hidden cost to mother and daughter for this work. Like the rays from radioactive elements, X-rays can also damage tissue and cause genetic mutations leading to cancer. The shielding used in the portable X-ray machines proved to be inadequate, and Marie's already heavy lifetime radiation exposure was increased by her wartime work. However, in the last two years of the war, about 1 million soldiers were X-rayed, saving many lives and allowing others to recover without becoming crippled.

By 1916, Marie had returned to the Radium Institute, where she set up a center to train women to become radiological assistants. As the German threat to France had receded, she also felt it safe to retrieve her precious gram of radium from Bordeaux. She used it to collect *radon* (the radioactive gas emitted by decaying radium) and seal it into little tubes. These tubes could be inserted by needle directly into the part of the body where diseased tissue needed to be destroyed. (Similar techniques are used today to destroy some prostate and other cancers.)

The war ended on November 11, 1918, but Marie worked nearly another year establishing radiological training and greatly contributing to the emergence of this medical specialty. She also wrote a book titled *Radiology in War* in which she told the story of her wartime work and explained its significance for medicine. Finally, she was able to go forward with her original research program for the Radium Institute.

CAMPAIGN FOR THE RADIUM INSTITUTE

For some time, Marie had developed a network of European industrialists and others who admired her work and were able to contribute financially. In 1920, she was able to extend her fund-raising across the Atlantic, thanks

(continues on page 68)

A DEADLY FAD

Not all uses of radium were medically appropriate or scientifically legitimate. By the early 20th century, radium's glow had penetrated deep into popular culture. Just as the (then-new) electricity had led 19th-century medical quacks to market all sorts of devices and treatments claiming to use electricity to heal or revitalize patients, radium too had its share of scams. Various brands of beauty creams and other cosmetic products claimed to be radium-enhanced—fortunately for their users, few of the products actually contained the costly element.

A more legitimate product was glow-in-the-dark paint, which could be made by adding a little radium to zinc sulfide and mixing it with a paint base. This paint was used for painting watches and instrument dials that could be read at night. Unfortunately, the workers, mostly women, who applied the radioactive paint were not warned of its dangers. They often moistened the tips of paintbrushes with their tongues.

Workers painting clock faces with radium. With no concern for their safety, many of these workers suffered from radiation sickness, brittle bones, and cancer. (*Photo by Daily Herald Archive / SSPL / Getty Images*)

By the mid-1920s, disturbing reports were coming from doctors and medical investigators. One dial painter had bleeding gums and unexplained bruises. A radiation counter chattered when brought near the dying patient, who it was found had inhaled radon. Other dial painters

(continues)

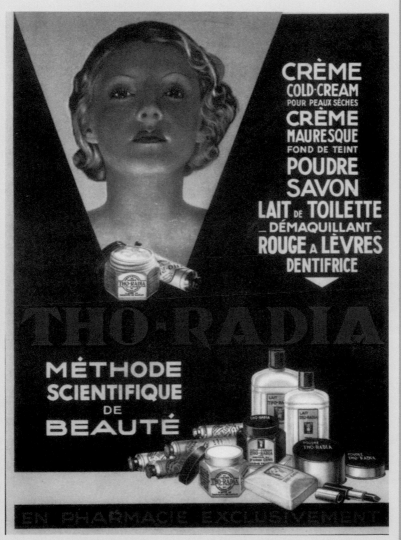

Cosmetics manufacturers began to tout radium as a new miracle ingredient. (*Musée Curie [Coll. ACJC]*)

(continued)

developed numerous bone fractures: many could no longer stand and were in danger of snapping their jaws if they even yawned. The United States Radium Company, the employer of many of the stricken women, settled a lawsuit out of court for only $13,000.

When she heard of such cases, Marie Curie was rather dismissive. She suggested that radium painters no longer lick their brushes—and that they eat calves liver to prevent anemia.

Today radioactive materials are tightly controlled, both for safety and to prevent access by terrorists. However, chances are good that a radioactive isotope called americium-241 is sitting right now in your house, perhaps right over your head. This extremely tiny bit of radioactivity is used to ionize the air passing through the most common type of smoke detector. This creates a small current that is interrupted if particles get in the way, indicating there may be a fire. The radiation in a smoke detector is harmless, but a broken detector should be returned to the manufacturer, which will dispose of it properly.

(continued from page 65)

to an interview with Marie Mattingly Meloney (1878–1943), editor of an American women's magazine called *The Delineator*. Meloney had built a career in journalism despite the fact that the field was largely a male domain. The Polish scientist and the American journalist soon found they had a mutual respect.

As she described her work to Meloney, Marie emphasized that despite being the discoverer of radium, her institution had only a single gram of the substance, while there were around 50 grams in the United States. Marie told Meloney that there was much she could do if she had only a single gram more of radium that could be used to generate radon gas for cancer treatment. Meloney was sympathetic to Marie's goals, as well as recognizing a splendid story.

Together, the two enterprising women organized something called the Marie Curie Radium Campaign. This campaign was organized primarily by women with wealth and social status and a number of distinguished American scientists. However, by the time $150,000 (a huge sum at the time) had been raised, many other women from all walks of life had pitched in. Meanwhile back in France, the Curie Foundation was established to provide funding and resources for the scientific and medical research work of the Radium Institute.

As part of the campaign, Meloney also arranged for Marie to write an autobiography. This book, though titled *Pierre Curie,* also included autobiographical notes that described Marie's own life and feelings. Overall, the book had a romantic and heroic tone—its theme was the struggle of Marie and Pierre to overcome not only the extreme difficulty of extracting radium but also the hostility and even outright opposition of the French scientific establishment.

The book exaggerated the Curies' hardships to some extent and, by portraying them as outsiders, minimized the help they had received from industrialists who later established a profitable radium industry. Nevertheless, the eloquent language appealed to many, particularly Americans (who had grown up reading about heroic inventors and businesspeople). No mention was made of the affair between Marie and Langevin, either in the book or in subsequent interviews in America. That story would remain unknown to most Americans.

In 1921, Meloney and her radium campaign committee arranged an American speaking tour for Marie. American audiences enthusiastically received her. A woman scientist was considered quite exotic at the time. She wore her usual black dress. After shaking hands with hundreds of people, she had to wear her right arm in a sling, and her daughters (particularly Irène) stood in for Marie at some of the gatherings, such as the awarding of numerous honorary degrees. (Irène dressed simply, even starkly, like her mother. The younger daughter, Eve, however, wore elegant fashions. One reporter, seeing Eve's eyes sparkle mischievously, called her "Miss Radium Eyes.")

One interesting stop for Marie was a tour of the factory in Canonsburg, Pennsylvania, that had produced the radium that she was about to be given. The amount of effort needed for its production went a long way to explain why the substance was so expensive. First, a team of about 300 men used shovels and dynamite to extract wagonloads of a radioactive ore called carnotite. The wagons were hauled 18 miles (29 km) by burro to a mill, where 500 tons (454 metric tons) of ore were chemically treated, pulverized, and mixed with powder. The treated product, in 100-pound (45-kg) sacks, then went 65 miles (105 km) to the railroad depot at Placerville, Colorado, for their final journey across country to the plant at Canonsburg.

After months of processing with acid and heat, the now-concentrated substance, reduced to a few hundred pounds, was sent to the Standard Chemical Company in Pittsburgh. After more months of additional processing the original 500 tons of ore yielded a few radium crystals, carefully kept in tubes within a lead-lined casket.

While tiring for Marie, this American trip and subsequent ones, as well as the international efforts to fund radium research, succeeded in placing the Radium Institute on a firm financial basis. Aided by Meloney's expertise, Marie had learned how to harness the media for her own purposes.

A WORLD CENTER

By the 1920s, the study of nuclear physics (the particles and interactions within the atom) had become an exciting field. Radioactivity was both a window into the atom and a tool for probing it. During its first 15 years (1919–34), scientists at the Radium Institute published 483 papers (including 31 publications by Marie herself).

While researchers at laboratories such as the Cavendish in Cambridge, England, and the Kaiser Wilhelm Institute in Germany focused on experiments in theoretical physics (such as the new quantum mechanics), Marie and the Radium Institute generally focused on more practical matters. They worked to isolate and produce commercial quantities of polonium and another important radioactive element, actinium.

Another important area for the Radium Institute was the establishment of standards for measuring radiation and methods for determining the actual radium content in products, medical or otherwise.

In later years, Marie did little research of her own, but that did not mean she was not intensely interested in every aspect of the Institute's work. She personally talked to each of the several dozen researchers in residence at any given time. A few of the researchers had a particular interest for Marie—fellow Poles and other women scientists.

Two researchers were of particular interest, and would achieve remarkable results leading to a Nobel Prize of their own. They were her daughter Irène and her husband Frédéric Joliot-Curie.

MARIE'S LAST YEARS

During the 1920s, Marie would continue to receive honors. One of the more remarkable ones came when the Academy of Medicine in Paris, urged by

Aged and ailing, Marie was still able to work with daughter Irène in the lab in 1927. *(AP Images)*

many members who had witnessed Marie's innovations in radium therapy, finally set aside its male-only status and elected her as a member.

The effects of cumulative radiation exposure continued to plague Marie. She suffered from cataracts (clouded lenses) in both eyes and required four operations to restore enough sight for her to be able to drive or work with laboratory instruments.

Although evidence of the dangerous effects of radiation slowly mounted, Marie seemed rather ambivalent if not in denial about how serious they could be. In 1925, Marie did participate in a commission of the French Academy of Medicine that recommended that lead screens be used to protect workers from radiation and that workers have regular blood tests to check for anemia (loss of oxygen-carrying red blood cells). Marie adopted the latter recommendation for researchers at the Radium Institute.

By the 1930s, Marie was chronically ill and often could not come to work at the lab. When at home she worked on her last book, *Radioactivity*. She also tried to watch her diet and exercise in fresh air.

In April 1934, Marie took an Easter trip with her sister Bronya and visited Pierre's brother, Jacques. In May, she became too ill to work at all.

Doctors at first through she might have tuberculosis and suggested she move to a sanitarium in Switzerland. Finally, a specialist from Geneva diagnosed her with aplastic pernicious anemia, a disease in which the bone marrow can no longer produce red blood cells. The disease was incurable at the time. (Today certain drugs or bone marrow transplants can be used successfully in many cases.)

Marie died on July 4, 1934. Two days later, she was buried in the cemetery in Sceaux where Pierre and her in-laws lay.

The Next Generation

Like Marie, her daughter Irène would meet someone who would be both her personal and scientific partner. Irène had absorbed all of the educational and scientific opportunities that came to the daughter of one of the world's most famous scientists. At the same time, according to biographer Eve Curie:

> The fame and the achievement of her parents neither discouraged nor intimidated her. . . . Her sincere love of science, her gifts, inspired in her only one ambition: to work forever in that laboratory which she had seen go up.

Irène adopted polonium as her main scientific project. Hard to isolate and quick to decay, polonium had been treated somewhat as radium's poor relation. Nevertheless, its high rate of activity made polonium a useful source of alpha particles for bombarding atoms in experiments.

THE NEW ASSISTANT

One day a new junior researcher arrived at the lab. Paul Langevin had mentored a promising student named Frédéric Joliot, who had graduated at the top of his class at the School of Physics and Chemistry (where Marie and Pierre Curie had made their radium discoveries).

As a boy Frédéric had been thrilled to read about heroic scientists such as the famous chemist Louis Pasteur and . . . Marie and Pierre Curie. The first meeting between Frédéric and his idol hardly seemed momentous: After grilling him about his modest educational qualifications, she asked him whether he could come to work the next morning. (He could, after receiving a dispensation from a colonel because he still had three weeks of military service to finish.)

Meanwhile Irène, fully established in the institute, had received her doctorate for her research on the radiation emitted by polonium. She was firmly focused on her work and took no particular interest at first in the inexperienced but energetic and outgoing Frédéric. He in turn seemed to regard Irène as formal, somewhat intimidating, and even a bit cold. Work however, threw them together. Marie sent Frédéric, who had no real experience with radiology, to Irène to be taught how to use the complicated and often unique apparatus the institute used to work with radioactive materials.

At first the relationship between the two was all business, but gradually Frédéric learned that Irène was not against having a good time—indeed, she often went dancing all night, only to arrive at the lab punctually at 8:00 A.M. The two young people also learned that they shared a love of sports and outdoor activities such as skiing and tennis. Soon they were walking home together across the Pont de la Tournelle Bridge across the Seine. Eventually weekend excursions were added.

A NEW FAMILY BEGINS

In March 1925, Irène defended her doctoral thesis on polonium before a packed audience at the Sorbonne. After receiving her degree, Marie joined her at a reception. A reporter from the French newspaper *Le Quotidien* approached with some questions for Irène. The woman reporter asked Irène whether she thought a woman could really manage a career working with dangerous radioactive materials. Irène replied that "I believe that men's and women's scientific aptitudes are exactly the same."

But what about children? Could a woman with such a career also meet her family duties? Irène replied that certainly it would be an added burden, but for her, science would always come first.

A new family was about to begin, however. Irène and Frédéric decided to marry. At first, Marie had her doubts about the strength of their relationship. She insisted on a prenuptial agreement and made sure that it would be Irène who would inherit control over the Institute's precious bit of radium. Frédéric and Irène were married on October 9, 1926, in a civil ceremony,

The couple was not given any particular financial support by Marie. Frédéric supplemented their income by doing some teaching. Despite the workload, he was also able to earn his doctorate (his dissertation was on the properties of polonium compounds).

The Joliot-Curies were now decently established scientifically, but Frédéric was uncertain about the future. In September 1927, their first child, Hélène, arrived. With another mouth to feed, Frédéric considered trying to find a better-paying job in industry. Fortunately for science, however, they continued to pursue their research into nuclear physics.

In 1929, Mattie Meloney visited Marie in Paris. Marie was, as always, anxious to obtain more precious radium. Mattie suggested to Marie that if she were willing to undertake another trip to America, enough money could be raised to buy another gram.

Marie agreed, though travel was getting to be hard for her. (Eve succeeded in getting her mother to buy a new dress for the occasion.) In October 1929, Marie was an overnight guest of President Herbert Hoover at the White House. She then met with the leading American industrialists—Henry Ford in Dearborn, Michigan, and Thomas Edison. Marie also won a major donation from General Electric.

MISSING THE NEUTRON

Meanwhile, Irène and Frédéric were working feverishly in the lab, seeking to learn more about the structure of the atom. Their most important tool was the alpha particles that spewed in great numbers from polonium. However polonium was very hard to extract, and the supply had to be continually renewed due to the element's short half-life.

Marie controlled the lab's polonium supply and determined how much each research team would receive. If the Joliot-Curies wanted more, they'd have to extract it themselves. Thus Frédéric and Irène alternated sessions of research with days devoted to the tedious, exacting, and dangerous process of extracting polonium, which involved the processing of highly radioactive solutions.

Their real research involved the systematic bombardment of substances whose atoms were prone to being jostled and releasing particles from their interiors. These particles could be identified by the tracks they left in a remarkable instrument, the Wilson *cloud chamber*. These tracks lasted only for a fraction of a second, but Frédéric devised a hookup with a camera that could snap pictures of the tracks, which could then be studied at leisure.

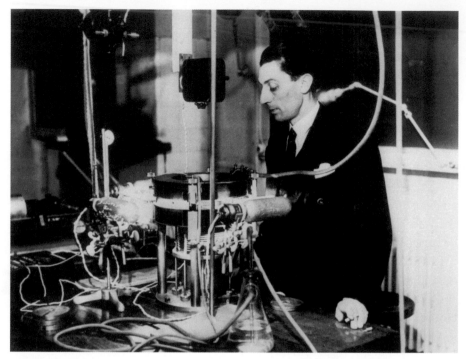

Frédéric Joliot-Curie with a Wilson cloud chamber. This device made it possible to photograph the tracks left by atomic particles. *(The Print Collector/Alamy)*

In 1930, a pair of German researchers, Walther Bothe and Herbert Becker, were also using polonium for nuclear bombardment. They were investigating what happens when emissions from a radioactive substance hit a nearby nonradioactive substance. When they bombarded the light element beryllium with a polonium radiation source, they found that what appeared to be a new kind of radiation was given off. It was so powerful that it could penetrate two cm (about an inch) into lead. Was it a more powerful kind of gamma ray or something else? The results puzzled the few dozen physicists around the world who were now doing nuclear experiments.

The following year, the Joliot-Curies were ready to perform the same experiment using the powerful polonium radiation source they had assembled. They exposed a plate of beryllium to the polonium rays. The result was radiation even more powerful than the German researchers had observed. When they placed a layer of paraffin (a substance containing hydrogen) on the other side of the beryllium, they observed what appeared (because of their mass) to be protons streaming out. In a preliminary report to the

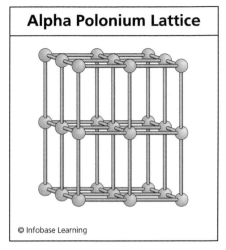

Alpha Polonium Lattice

© Infobase Learning

The short half-life of polonium made it hard to obtain a pure sample and identify its crystal form.

French Academy, the Joliot-Curies announced, "The Emission of Protons of High Velocity from Hydrogenous Materials Irradiated with Very Penetrating Gamma Rays."

Other physicists were dubious that something as heavy as a proton could be displaced by the gamma rays from the beryllium. Ernest Rutherford said he doubted that what the Joliot-Curies had tracked were really protons, but they had clearly found something.

At the Cavendish Laboratory, another researcher James Chadwick (1891–1974) told Ernest Rutherford about the Joliot-Curies' proton theory. Rutherford said that he simply did not believe it. Rutherford and Chadwick knew that Irène and Frédéric were careful researchers. They assumed their observations were correct—it was the interpretation that was in question.

Back in 1920, Rutherford had suggested that the behavior of atomic nuclei when bombarded with alpha particles might be better explained by the existence of an additional particle about the size of the proton but without an electric charge. He called this hypothetical particle a *neutron.*

In February 1932, Chadwick began an intensive series of experiments in an attempt to identify the true nature of the particles. After confirming the Joliot-Curies' results using paraffin, he bombarded a succession of other substances with the radiation from the polonium-beryllium interaction. In each case, he observed a similar number of protons being forcefully ejected from the paraffin target. Since the radiation that was doing this seemed to be able to easily penetrate atoms without being deflected by their negatively charged electrons, Chadwick concluded that the radiation was none other than Rutherford's neutron.

The resulting paper, directly challenging the Joliot-Curie proton theory, caused an uproar (and upset Marie considerably). By April, however, Frédéric had conceded that Chadwick was right. The Joliot-Curies had missed out on the discovery of the neutron, which would gain Chadwick a Nobel Prize.

The neutron was a key part of the atomic puzzle. Neutrons, together with protons, make up the nucleus of the atom. Because of their ability to penetrate the nucleus without being repelled by its electrical charge, energetic neutrons could be used in experiments that would revolutionize nuclear physics, leading to nuclear fission and the atomic age.

ANOTHER NEAR MISS

Radiation and stress were taking their toll on Irène, but she refused to let the demands of her body get in the way of their research. Nuclear physics had become a race to discover new particles, and Frédéric, writing to a friend (as recounted in a biography by Maurice Goldsmith), had complained:

> We have been working very hard. . . . We had to speed up the pace of our experiments for it is annoying to be overtaken by other laboratories which immediately take up one's experiments . . . as was done in Cambridge.

Irène's health did not improve. After several brief visits to a Swiss sanatorium, she was finally diagnosed with tuberculosis. This infectious lung disease was one of the most insidious killers of the era before antibiotics. It was unpredictable: It could kill in months or sap a person's strength for years. Frédéric responded by taking a greater share of their already backbreaking workload.

By this time they, like other nuclear physicists, were trying to find out everything one could do with the newly identified neutron. The Joliot-Curies found themselves looking at another aspect of the polonium-alpha-proton collision puzzle. Using the cloud chamber, they could see the tracks of electrons that were also whizzing about as a result of the collisions. One time, they observed the track of an electron that seemed to be going the wrong way. Instead of moving outward from the radiation source, it was headed inward! They published their photograph of the mysterious wrong-way electron.

It was a few months later that they learned that Carl Anderson (1905–91), a researcher at Caltech in Pasadena, California, had already identified the nature of the wrong-way electron. It was a particle the same size as an electron, but positively rather than negatively charged—a positron.

Looking back at their photographs, the Joliot-Curies found an example of an electron and positron track coming together. The two oppositely charged particles annihilated each other when they collided, releasing a burst of energy—in fact, a gamma ray. (The positron was the first example of an antiparticle to be found. Eventually anti-counterparts of most of the other particles would be found.)

Their publication of the new electron-positron photo was a bit of a consolation prize, but again the Joliot-Curies had made an error of interpretation. Their reputation was starting to suffer, and discouragement began to set in.

Over that summer, the Joliot-Curies took part in an excursion to the Soviet Union. Interested in social and educational reform, they went with Langevin and some other scientists to visit some Soviet scientists. Like many Western liberals and leftists of the 1930s, they had come to feel that only the growing Soviet power could restrain the already evident menace of German Nazism. The Soviets also seemed to offer a social model that was more just and humane than capitalism, which had brought the crushing poverty of the Great Depression of the 1930s.

As with their recent particle experiments, however, what Frédéric and Irène saw in the Soviet Union was not what it seemed. The scientists they met were carefully selected by the Soviet government. The laboratories and schools and the working and living conditions were far from those experienced by typical Soviet workers. They, like other Western visitors who returned with glowing reports of the Soviet experiment, had seen only what they were meant to see. Only later would Stalin's purges, deliberate famines, and notorious Gulag labor camps become known in the West.

A NEW PROTON THEORY

As they got back to physics, the Joliot-Curies came up with a new theory based on their recent observations. They issued a paper titled "Penetrating Radiation from Atoms Bombarded by Alpha Rays" in which they said that when they had bombarded lighter elements such as boron or aluminum with alpha rays they had detected a mixture of protons, neutrons, and electrons. They believed that in some cases instead of a proton being emitted, a combination of a neutron and a positron could be seen. Frédéric then made a startling assertion: The proton may not be an elementary particle at all, but rather a composite of two other particles—such as a neutron and a positron!

In 1933, the Joliot-Curies attended the annual Solvay conference in Brussels. Neutrons and controversy were in the air. Among the distinguished physicists was Lise Meitner (1878–1968), a formidable physicist sometimes called "the German Marie Curie." Meitner said that she and colleagues at the prestigious Kaiser Wilhelm Institute in Berlin had tried to reproduce the Joliot-Curies' most recent experiments without success. Further, their composite proton theory seemed dubious to most other nuclear physicists.

Were they on the wrong track? The doubts that began to creep into Frédéric and Irène's minds were relieved only by Niels Bohr (1885–1962), the

LISE MEITNER AND NUCLEAR FISSION

Until the latter part of the 20th century, Marie Curie was just about the only woman scientist that one could guarantee virtually everyone had heard of. However, science writers and historians then began to pay attention to another woman physicist who was well known in her field, if not by the general public.

Lise Meitner (1878–1968) was born in Vienna, Austria, to a Jewish family that valued education—but girls were not sent to college. Young Lise, having read about Marie Curie's work, wanted to become a physicist. A change in educational policy allowed her to apply to the university, but she and other girls had to scramble to make up for the inadequacy of their early education, which was more suited for working in a shop or factory.

In 1901, Meitner was accepted by the University of Vienna; in 1906, she enrolled in the University of Berlin for graduate study in physics. There she ran into a wall of prejudice: Women were not allowed to use the laboratory, so she and a friendly colleague, Otto Hahn, set up a small lab of their own in the basement carpentry shop.

After graduation, Meitner and Hahn became an effective scientific team—Meitner was strong in physical theory and mathematics, while Hahn was an excellent chemist. Carefully studying the beta particles (electrons) produced by radioactive decay, Meitner determined that they were actually being created within the nucleus of the atom itself, rather than being stripped from the outer orbits.

Meitner's growing scientific stature could not save her, a Jew, from the rise of Nazi Germany, which in 1938 forcibly annexed Austria.

imposing Danish theoretical physicist whose quantum theories had established the modern scientific picture of the atom. As quoted in Pierre Biquard's biography of Frédéric, Bohr told them that "what you are doing is of the greatest importance."

While this encouragement probably helped, the track record of the Joliot-Curies was not looking good. With their latest theory in ruins, they could only go back to work and see if they could find something that could stand up.

Meitner's friends helped her find a lightly guarded border crossing through which she was able to escape to the Netherlands and then to Sweden, where the great nuclear theoretician Niels Bohr offered her work.

Meanwhile, in Berlin Otto Hahn and his assistant Fritz Strassman were using neutrons for an effective new kind of atomic bombardment. (Neutrons, lacking electric charge, were better able to hit an atomic nucleus without being diverted.) Bombarding uranium, Hahn and Strassman thought that they had "chipped" away a bit of the uranium nucleus to yield radium, which was four *atomic numbers* lower. Unfortunately the numbers did not add up: an alpha particle (two protons) should only have reduced the number by two.

When these puzzling results arrived in Denmark, Meitner and her nephew, the physicist Otto Frisch, were intrigued. Based on her knowledge of the behavior of uranium atoms, Meitner came up with a bold idea: the bombarded uranium nucleus had not been chipped down to a radium one. Rather, it had been split in two—one piece of which was barium (number 56), an element that, as the Curies had learned, was chemically almost identical to radium! Meitner suggested that this phenomenon of splitting atoms be called nuclear *fission*.

In 1944, Otto Hahn was awarded the Nobel Prize for the discovery of nuclear fission. Ever since, Lise Meitner's supporters have argued that she, too, should have shared in that prize. This opinion was supported by a study conducted in 1997 by the magazine *Physics Today*. The newly discovered element number 107 was named meitnerium in her honor.

ATOMIC ALCHEMY

One day in January 1934 Frédéric exposed an aluminum target to the radiation from a polonium source as a *Geiger counter* chattered nearby. As he withdrew the radiation source, he of course expected the chattering to die down and then stop. Instead, the instrument kept registering radiation, even though the polonium was no longer present. Only after several minutes did the radiation count subside to background levels.

Rushing to get Irène, Frédéric told her what had happened. Had they somehow created a new source of radiation? They knew they had to check their instruments carefully, especially the newly developed (and delicate) Geiger counter. They also had to rule out any source of contamination—some bit of radioactive material that had gotten in somehow. It would not do to rush out with yet another theory, only to have it shot down.

That weekend the Joliot-Curies had a colleague check the Geiger counter independently—it was functioning fine. They also stopped a fellow researcher who was going home and persuaded him to run the experiment himself so

Irène and Frédéric at work in their lab in 1934, the year they discovered how to produce artificial radioactivity. *(Popperfoto/Getty Images)*

Artificial Radioactivity

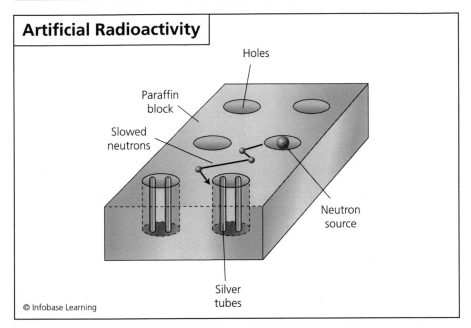

Holes

Paraffin
block

Slowed
neutrons

Neutron
source

© Infobase Learning

Silver
tubes

As discovered by the Joliot-Curies in 1934, neutrons at the correct speed can be absorbed by atoms (silver in this case) to create a radioactive isotope.

that there would be independent evidence of the mysterious persistence of radiation.

As their excitement grew, Frédéric and Irène sent for Marie and also invited Paul Langevin to the lab. They conferred, checked, and double-checked. The following Monday there would be a regular meeting of the French Academy of Sciences. Quickly, they wrote up their report, giving it the title "A New Type of Radioactivity."

Their claim was sensational. Evidence would be demanded and carefully scrutinized by physicists around the world. The Joliot-Curies knew that a new radioactive substance must have been created in the aluminum by the bombardment from the polonium. However, the fact that the Geiger counter's clicking died away after only about three minutes meant that this new radioactivity was short-lived.

Somehow they had to isolate and document this new *radioisotope* in only three minutes. Frédéric took charge of the bombardment, then quickly sealed the irradiated aluminum. Irène, using the techniques she had learned from her mother so many years ago, separated out the new radioactive substance—an isotope of phosphorus.

When they had a tiny vial of the substance, Irène pressed it into the radiation-scarred hand of her ailing mother. Marie had lived just long enough to see her daughter and son-in-law make a momentous discovery. Radioactive substances could be created!

When the calculations were worked out, physicists could see what had happened. Aluminum has an atomic number of 13 (meaning that it has 13 protons in its nucleus). The alpha particles emitted by the polonium consisted of two protons and two neutrons each. If an alpha particle happened to hit an aluminum atom in the right way, its two protons were absorbed into the aluminum nucleus, raising its atomic number to 15. That made it a new element, phosphorus. But because it was not a stable configuration, the phosphorus was radioactive and soon decayed.

This discovery, called nuclear transmutation, would prove to be very significant. On a practical level, it led to the development of ways to create artificial radioactive isotopes for use in medicine and industry without needing to resort to the tedious and expensive process of extracting elements such as radium from ores.

(continues on page 88)

Isotopes of Hydrogen

Hydrogen
One proton

Deuterium
One proton,
one neutron

Tritium
One proton,
two neutrons

© Infobase Learning

Isotopes are variants of an element that have different numbers of neutrons in the nucleus.

Radium Decay Chain

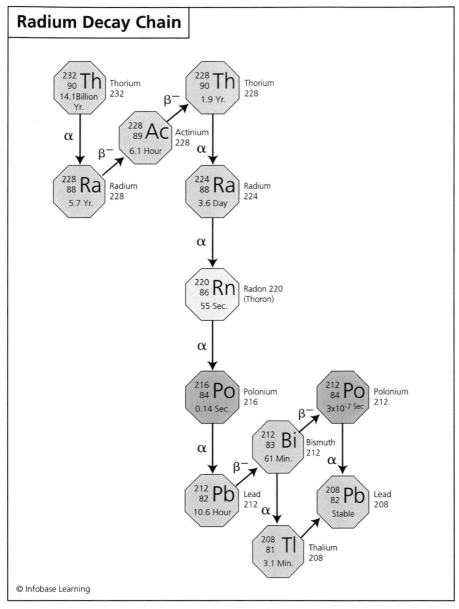

© Infobase Learning

Some radioactive elements, such as radium, go through a series of transformations as the atoms break down. In the chart, the atomic number is shown to the upper left of the element symbol and the number in the lower left is the atomic weight (the number of protons). For example, thorium (atomic number 90, atomic weight 232) can emit an alpha particle (atomic number 2, atomic weight 4) and become radium (atomic number 88, atomic weight 228).

RISE OF THE ATOM SMASHERS

In the early years of nuclear research, the only way to obtain energetic particles for bombarding atoms was by using the natural emissions from radioactive elements such as polonium. This approach had drawbacks: It required expensive and potentially hazardous radioactive materials, and the particles had limited energy. Without a source of more energetic particles, the advance of nuclear physics probably would have stalled by the late 1930s.

Fortunately, a number of approaches were developed for creating more and more powerful particles to serve as atomic bullets in experiments. A basic approach is to use a high-voltage electrical discharge to propel charged particles or ions. A more advanced form of this linear accelerator uses oscillating (rapidly changing) electrical charges to pump the charged particles to higher and higher energies. Producing a moderate energy (tens of millions of electron volts), this type of accelerator is used today mainly for medical radiotherapy.

Linear accelerators like this Cockroft-Walton unit at Fermilab can be used alone for medical therapy or as the first stage of a larger accelerator. *(Fermilab)*

Perhaps the best-known type of accelerator is the circular *cyclotron*. After injecting the particles at high energy using a Tesla coil or Van De Graf generator, magnets bend the path of the particles as they are accelerated continuously. The development of cyclotrons by Ernest O. Lawrence (1901–58) at the University of California, Berkeley, in the 1930s marked the entry of the United States as a new player in the race to unlock atomic secrets. These devices were popularly known as atom smashers, although much of the research per-

Modern particle accelerators can be huge, with their circular tracks running underground. Shown here from the air at Fermilab are the main injector in the foreground and the Tevatron in the back. *(Fermilab)*

formed with them dealt with interactions between subatomic particles, not whole atoms.

Cyclotrons and the more advanced synchrotrons were developed throughout the latter half of the 20th century. While early particle accelerators were usually used to bombard a fixed target with electrons, protons, or ions, the most powerful type of accelerator today is the collider, where two beams are generated, accelerated in opposite directions, and then slammed into each other at extremely high energy.

The Large Hadron Collider (LHC) is the world's largest and most powerful particle accelerator. Located in a tunnel deep beneath the border between Switzerland and France, the LHC is a ring 17 miles (27 km) in circumference. It contains 1,232 dipole magnets that are used to propel the two opposing beams on their separate, parallel paths, while another 392 quadrapole magnets are used to keep the beams focused. (The magnets,

(continues)

(continued)

which must be kept extremely cold using liquid helium, generally weigh 27 tons [24.5 metric tons] each.)

This massive project was developed through the combined efforts of more than 10,000 scientists and engineers from more than 100 countries. It is operated by CERN, the European Organization for Nuclear Research.

After some initial mishaps, the LHC began full-scale operations in 2010. Protons are now being smashed together at energies of 14 TeV (trillion electron volts) or more. Researchers hope that the immense energies, comparable to those found in the very earliest moments of the universe, will provide proof of particles such as the Higgs boson (responsible for mass), predicted by the Standard Model of particle physics.

(continued from page 84)

But the discovery that changes could be induced in the very heart of an atom would suggest something else as well—that atoms could be made to fission, or split apart. That line of thought would lead to nuclear reactors and the atomic bomb.

In 1935, the Joliot-Curies were awarded the Nobel Prize in chemistry. (This made Irène only the second woman to win a Nobel.) In his Nobel lecture, Frédéric made a prediction based on what was being observed when uranium was subjected to the kind of bombardment they had been doing with lighter elements:

If we look at the past and consider the progress made by science at an ever increasing pace, we may feel entitled to believe that researchers, building up or breaking down elements at will, will be able to bring about nuclear reactions of an explosive nature—veritable chain reactions [and] one can imagine the enormous release of useful energy which will take place.

Frédéric went on to express the belief, shared by some other physicists, that chain reactions could get out of control and even convert the whole Earth to energy in a supernova-like flash. While this fear proved to be unfounded, what nuclear weapons actually could do would prove to be devastating enough.

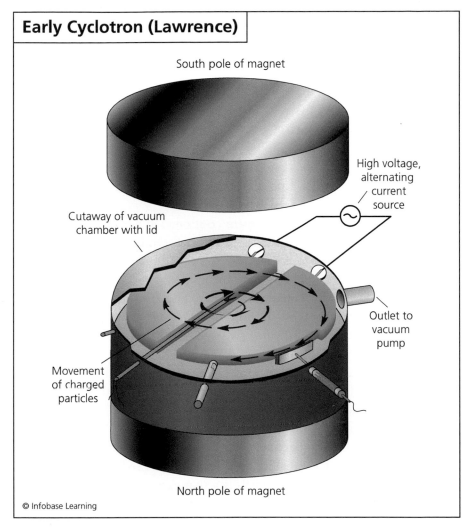

Early Cyclotron (Lawrence)

South pole of magnet

High voltage, alternating current source

Cutaway of vacuum chamber with lid

Outlet to vacuum pump

Movement of charged particles

North pole of magnet

© Infobase Learning

Developed in the 1930s by Ernest O. Lawrence, the cyclotron, a circular particle accelerator, allowed researchers to generate and control beams of particles for bombarding target substances.

The prestige gained from the Nobel Prize led to Irène being appointed to a chair at the Sorbonne. Frédéric, too, took on important research, teaching, and administrative work.

ATOMS SPLIT AND FRANCE FALLS

The exciting but stressful months of discovery had again taken a toll on Irène. She was in and out of the sanatorium, each time being told that she could return to work "in moderation." But moderation was not something Curies did. She always returned to the lab sooner than recommended, though she did have a cot put in her office so she could take the occasional nap.

Irène also became increasingly involved in political issues—rights for women and workers and the need to fight the growing fascism that had taken hold in Germany and Spain.

In 1938, Irène accepted the position of undersecretary for scientific research for the liberal-socialist French government. By then, the power of Nazi Germany had grown into an imminent threat to France, as well as Marie's native Poland.

Meanwhile Frédéric's research team continued its work on nuclear bombardment. Some of their results (which Frédéric could not quite interpret), along with the work of Otto Hahn in Berlin, found their way to two German scientists, Otto Frisch and Lise Meitner, who had fled the Nazis. Meitner recognized the true significance of what had happened. Atoms had actually been split apart by neutron bombardment. Using Einstein's famous formula $E=mc^2$, she calculated the immense energy that could be yielded by nuclear fission.

Frédéric in turn began to explore fission and the possibility of causing fissions to trigger further fissions (a chain reaction). In April 1939, the Joliot research group published a report in the publication *Nature* outlining what was known about nuclear chain reactions.

As word spread about the explosive potential of nuclear fission and chain reactions, one physicist, a Hungarian refugee named Leó Szilárd, wrote a letter to Frédéric, warning of the possibility that extremely dangerous fission weapons might end up in the hands of the Nazis. When Frédéric did not respond, Szilard took his concerns elsewhere, enlisting the support of Albert Einstein and leading on August 2 to a famous warning letter sent to the American president, Franklin D. Roosevelt. (This in turn became a major impetus to the American atom bomb project.)

In May 1940, the Germans invaded France. This time there would be no miraculous fleet of taxicabs coming to the defense of Paris. Moving with unprecedented speed, German armored forces backed by dive-bombers cut deeply into France. By the middle of June, France had been defeated and came firmly under German control. Northern France (including Paris) and the Atlantic coast would be governed directly by the Germans, while the remainder, in the south, would have a puppet government based in the city of Vichy.

WARTIME RESISTANCE

By September, Frédéric was back in his laboratory, trying to work, not knowing what the Germans might decide to do with him. Suddenly, a German, Erich Schumann, arrived at the lab. He was a general, a physicist, and a composer (a descendant of Robert Schumann, the famous 19th-century composer).

Surprisingly, at first the general greeted Frédéric and the lab staff with friendly words of praise for their work. The Germans were anxious to find the supply of uranium and heavy water (water with hydrogen atoms that contained neutrons) that could be used for creating a nuclear reactor.

Frédéric tried to maneuver carefully between defying the Germans (which would have led to his losing control of the lab and probable arrest) and actively collaborating with them. He told the general where he thought the nuclear materials had been moved, but that he did not know what had happened to them.

Frédéric apparently tried to convince the Germans to let the lab continue to operate as a pure theoretical research facility, but it remains unclear to this day whether some of their wartime work may have helped the German military. At any rate, it became clear after the war that the Germans had conducted only limited and uncoordinated nuclear research and had never achieved a controlled nuclear chain reaction.

Whatever compromises he may have made, Frédéric's personal courage was considerable. When Paul Langevin (now 68 years old) was arrested by the Gestapo, the auditorium where he was scheduled to give a lecture was locked. Hundreds of Sorbonne students gathered outside the doors. Frédéric then arrived, strode past the students and the guards, pulled a key out of his pocket, and opened the room.

As the auditorium filled with students and overflowed outside, Frédéric walked to the podium and announced that he was closing his laboratory and suspending classes until Langevin was released. (More than a month later, Langevin was released from jail but taken to a remote village in the south of France and kept under house arrest.)

Frédéric continued to publicly defy the Germans. He organized and joined student demonstrations against the occupiers. He also eventually reopened the laboratory. However, his main effort would be to secretly aid the French resistance.

In the following years, Frédéric was occasionally arrested and questioned but then released. (The fact that he seemed to be untouchable led to rumors that he was a Nazi collaborator.) Meanwhile, Irène continued to struggle with tuberculosis and went to Switzerland to recover. She periodically went back to Nazi-occupied France to visit with Frédéric and their children, though this was risky, and sometimes she was stopped by police.

Meanwhile Eve, the younger Curie daughter, had fled to England, where her ship came under German fire crossing the Channel. Eve already had a reputation from her best-selling biography of Marie. She easily moved in British society, meeting Winston Churchill. She also went to America, met Eleanor Roosevelt, and gave lectures and interviews about the situation in France and the role of French women.

Eve joined the Free French forces under Charles de Gaulle and became a war correspondent. She observed the military campaign in North Africa and Egypt and visited parts of the Middle East and Asia, as well as the Soviet Union.

LIBERATION

Finally, following the successful D-day invasion in June 1944, Allied forces advanced toward Paris. This was the signal for the resistance fighters in Paris, joined by much of the French police, to take up arms and attack the German garrison. The poorly trained and equipped resistance fighters were at a disadvantage as German tanks rolled into the streets of Paris.

Down the street came Frédéric with two heavy suitcases. Ducking into a friend's laboratory, he was joined by two other men. In the cellar was a supply of champagne that had belonged to a German collaborator. Quickly they emptied each bottle, replacing the beverage with a mixture of gasoline and sulfuric acid taken from the suitcases. The bottles were then wrapped in paper impregnated with potassium chlorate. The explosive Molotov cocktails were now ready to pass to the waiting fighters. As author Robert Jungk points out in his account *Brighter Than a Thousand Sons,* "The man who had discovered some of the most necessary pre-conditions for the construction of the atom bomb [was] using the most primitive form of bomb imaginable in defense of the barricades."

Primitive though they might be, the firebombs could be quite effective. German tank crews had to keep their hatches shut, lest they be incinerated by one of the improvised weapons. As the fighting raged on, the German commander, who was very fond of Paris and did not want to see the city destroyed, secretly agreed to let the approaching Americans enter the city. They did, but out of respect for the French, the Americans allowed a Free French division to enter first.

COLD WAR YEARS

Following the liberation of France, Frédéric, who had tried to deflect the suspicions of German interrogators, now faced American ones. American intelligence officers were suspicious of the role the Joliot-Curies and their lab might have played during the war. How much might they have helped the Germans?

A special intelligence unit also became involved. It had been organized by Leslie Groves, the American general in charge of the Manhattan Project. Groves badly wanted to know what progress the Germans might have made in nuclear research during the war.

When detained for questioning, Frédéric told the Americans that the Germans who worked at the lab had done little of consequence. He insisted his own work was without any military application. When it became clear that the Joliot-Curies had communist leanings, it perhaps became less credible in the Americans' minds that they would have collaborated with the Nazis. On the other hand, it was already beginning to look like the Soviet Union would become the next great enemy of the West.

INTO THE ATOMIC AGE

The postwar period brought Frédéric many honors. He was appointed director of the National Center for Scientific Research as well as being elected to the French Academy of Sciences. It was clear that atomic energy would play a vital part in the postwar world. A nation that did not have its own nuclear program might well be regarded as a second-class power. France, under nationalist leader Charles de Gaulle, was determined to avoid this fate.

The Joliot-Curies were intended to play a key role in France's nuclear ambitions. In 1945, Frédéric was appointed head of the French Atomic Energy Commission. Irène was also appointed to the commission, as well as becoming director of the Radium Institute.

By this time nuclear physics was on its way to becoming an industry, with the first nuclear reactors being built for research and the eventual production of what was hoped to be abundant, inexpensive energy. Frédéric played a key role in the design and development of ZOE, France's first nuclear reactor.

However the Joliot-Curies' politics proved to be a problem for the French authorities. While the elder Curies had been liberal, the younger couple were rather more radical—socialist, with communist leanings. (In 1942, Frédéric

Irène Joliot-Curie is shown at a press conference introducing ZOE, France's first nuclear reactor, designed by Frédéric Joliot-Curie. *(Keystone/Getty Images)*

had joined the French Communist Party, which was part of the anti-Nazi coalition.)

In nuclear matters, the United States had a great deal of influence, and, with the cold war underway, the message was clear: Communists or suspected communists must be removed from sensitive posts. Both Frédéric and Irène were dismissed from their positions on the Atomic Energy Commission in 1950.

Frédéric was far from apologetic about his beliefs. If anything, he became an even more committed communist in the 1950s. He did retain his university post (and "inherited" Irène's after her death). In 1955, Frédéric joined Albert Einstein and logician and philosopher Bertrand Russell (1872–1970) in signing a manifesto calling for world peace and an end to the stockpiling of nuclear weapons. Frédéric died only two years after Irène on August 14, 1958.

When the war ended, Irène remained active in women's education and women's rights. She was also active in the World Peace Council, a nonaligned organization that was actually funded by the Soviet Union as a propaganda tool.

In 1956, Irène contracted leukemia, a type of blood cancer that can also be caused by radiation exposure. She died on March 17, 1956.

Eve Curie became a minister for women's affairs in the de Gaulle government. She was also an adviser to NATO. She married the American diplomat Henry Richardson Labouisse, Jr., and, along with him, served in a number of important positions with the United Nations, notably with the United Nations Children's Fund (UNICEF).

Unlike the radium-scarred Marie and Irène, Eve lived a remarkably long life. In 2005, in recognition of her work with UNICEF, she was given France's highest decoration, being made an officer of the Legion of Honor. She died on October 22, 2007, at the age of 102.

Conclusion

For most of the 20th century, Marie Curie was an icon, *the* woman scientist, the example given to every bright girl of what might be possible if she worked hard enough. As noted in *Madame Curie,* Albert Einstein once remarked: "Marie Curie is, of all celebrated beings, the one whom fame has not corrupted."

In his biography of Marie Curie, Robert Reid noted that:

> As a woman scientist she was liberated because she had created the conditions for her own liberation. She had tackled her profession's problems as an equal to all the rest involved; and all the rest happened to be men. She had expected no concessions and none had been made. She had survived because she had made men believe they were dealing not just with an equal, but also with an intensive equal.

However her seeming uniqueness, together with the pedestal that some biographers (starting with Eve) seemed to erect for her, sometimes made it hard to see her as a brilliant, dedicated human being with her share of human flaws.

As time passed, Marie Curie has become less unique in some ways. Starting with her daughter Irène, Marie has been joined by nine other women at the Nobel Prize rostrum. Women may still be not proportionally represented in the highest echelons of science, but brilliant and competent woman scientists are no longer considered unusual. Marie's lessening uniqueness is a lasting tribute to the effect her life has had on so many young women.

In an introduction to a new edition of Eve Curie's biography *Madame Curie,* science writer Natalie Angier writes that:

> . . . in a sense Madame Curie was the mother of us all, a role model for every girl who stakes a claim to a life of the mind, particularly that part of the mind too often deemed masculine—the scientific, mathematical part. I have interviewed hundreds of female scientists over the years, and a number of them have told me how, in their girlhood, the story of Madame Curie captivated and inspired them. Through reading about her, they felt less freakish, less alone in their passionate "unfeminine" love of algebra and chemistry kits.

An indication of the lasting respect for Marie Curie came in 1995, when both Marie and Pierre were reinterred in the Panthéon, France's national mausoleum. In his address at the ceremony, French president François Mitterand (dying of cancer) made a statement that seems rather apologetic:

> As the country bows before her ashes . . . I form the wish, in the name of France, that everywhere in the world the equality of the rights of women and men might progress.

Mitterand went on to note that:

> By transferring these ashes of Pierre and Marie Curie into the sanctuary of our collective memory, France not only performs an act of recognition, it also affirms a faith in science, in research, and its respect for those who dedicate themselves to science, just as Pierre and Marie Curie dedicated their energies and their lives to science.

(Scientists testing Marie's remains with a Geiger counter were surprised to find that they were less radioactive then expected. They concluded that it was likely not radium that had killed her, but overexposure to X-rays during her wartime ambulance service.)

Poland, Marie's native land, has also paid her special tribute. In 1998, a conference was held in Warsaw honoring the 100th anniversary of the Curies' discovery of polonium and radium. Participating scientists came

The first giant magnets installed at the LHC at CERN—by 2010 the huge facility was online, creating unprecedented energies. (© *Maximilien Brice/CERN*)

from 13 countries and included 12 Nobel Prize winners. The audience included Hélène Langevin-Joliot (granddaughter of Marie Curie). During 2011, a special celebration was held honoring the 100th anniversary of Marie Curie's 1911 Nobel Prize in chemistry.

The ultimate legacy of Marie, Pierre, Irène, and Frédéric, however, lies not just in the honors they have been given, but also in what their work, often, at great personal cost, has enabled us to learn about the very atoms we are made of. Their work, along with that of other first- and second-generation nuclear physicists, established the experimental approaches and fashioned the instruments needed to probe the subatomic world. Just as the spirit of Galileo's little spyglass lives on in the universe-spanning *Hubble Space Telescope,* the Curies' probes into the heart of matter find their descendant in the city-sized LHC.

Periodic Table of the Elements

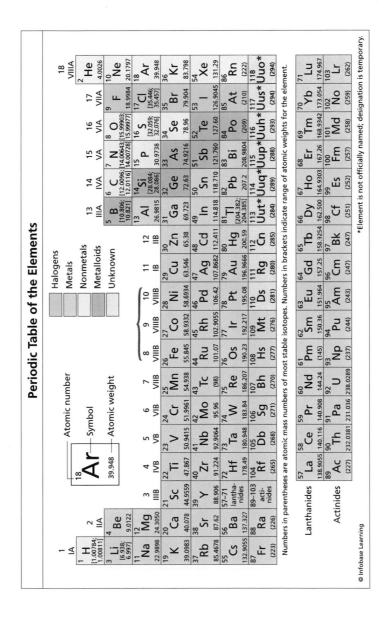

Periodic Table of the Elements

Numbers in parentheses are atomic mass numbers of most stable isotopes. Numbers in brackets indicate range of atomic weights for the element.

*Element is not officially named; designation is temporary.

© Infobase Learning

The Chemical Elements

(g) none (c) nonmetallics

element	symbol	a.n.
carbon	C	6
hydrogen	H	1

(g) chalcogen (c) nonmetallics

element	symbol	a.n.
oxygen	O	8
polonium	Po	84
selenium	Se	34
sulfur	S	16
tellurium	Te	52
ununhexium	Uuh	116

(g) alkali metal (c) metallics

element	symbol	a.n.
cesium	Cs	55
francium	Fr	87
lithium	Li	3
potassium	K	19
rubidium	Rb	37
sodium	Na	11

(g) alkaline earth metal (c) metallics

element	symbol	a.n.
barium	Ba	56
beryllium	Be	4
calcium	Ca	20
magnesium	Mg	12
radium	Ra	88
strontium	Sr	38

(g) none (c) metallics

element	symbol	a.n.	element	symbol	a.n.
aluminum	Al	13	scandium	Sc	21
bohrium	Bh	107	seaborgium	Sg	106
cadmium	Cd	48	silver	Ag***	47
chromium	Cr	24	tantalum	Ta	73
cobalt	Co	27	technetium	Tc	43
copper	Cu***	29	thallium	Tl	81
darmstadtium	Ds	110	titanium	Ti	22
dubnium	Db	105	tin	Sn	50
gallium	Ga	31	tungsten	W	74
gold	Au***	79	ununbium	Uub	112
hafnium	Hf	72	ununtrium	Uut	113
hassium	Hs	108	ununquadium	Uuq	114
indium	In	49	vanadium	V	23
iridium	Ir*****	77	yttrium	Y	39
iron	Fe	26	zinc	Zn	30
lawrencium	Lr	103	zirconium	Zr	40
lead	Pb	82			
lutetium	Lu	71			
manganese	Mn	25			
meitnerium	Mt	109			
mercury	Hg	80			
molybdenum	Mo	42			
nickel	Ni	28			
niobium	Nb	41			
osmium	Os*****	76			
palladium	Pd*****	46			
platinum	Pt*****	78			
rhenium	Re	75			
rhodium	Rh*****	45			
roentgenium	Rg	111			
ruthenium	Ru*****	44			
rutherfordium	Rf	104			

(g) pnictogen (c) metallics

element	symbol	a.n.
arsenic	As*	33
antimony	Sb*	51
bismuth	Bi	83
nitrogen	N	7
phosophorus	P**	15
ununpentium	Uup	115

(g) none (c) semimetallics

element	symbol	a.n.
boron	B	5
germanium	Ge	32
silicon	Si	14

(g) actinoid (c) metallics

element	symbol	a.n.
actinium	Ac	89
americium	Am	95
berkelium	Bk	97
californium	Cf	98
curium	Cm	96
einsteinium	Es	99
fermium	Fm	100
mendelevium	Md	101
neptunium	Np	93
nobelium	No	102
plutonium	Pu	94
protactinium	Pa	91
thorium	Th	90
uranium	U	92

(g) halogens (c) nonmetallics

element	symbol	a.n.
astatine	At*	85
bromine	Br	35
chlorine	Cl	17
fluorine	F	9
iodine	I	53
ununseptium	Uus*	117

(g) lanthanoid (c) metallics

element	symbol	a.n.
cerium	Ce	58
dysprosium	Dy	66
erbium	Er	68
europium	Eu	63
gadolinium	Gd	64
holmium	Ho	67
lanthanum	La	57
neodymium	Nd	60
praseodymium	Pr	59
promethium	Pm	61
samarium	Sm	62
terbium	Tb	65
thulium	Tm	69
ytterbium	Yb	70

(g) noble gases (c) nonmetallics

element	symbol	a.n.
argon	Ar	18
helium	He	2
krypton	Kr	36
neon	Ne	10
radon	Rn	86
xenon	Xe	54
ununoctium	Uuo	118

* = semimetallics (c)
** = nonmetallics (c)
*** = coinage metal (g)
**** = precious metal (g)

a.n. = atomic number
(g) = group
(c) = classification

Chronology

May 15, 1859
Pierre Curie is born in Paris, France

November 7, 1867
Marie Skłodowska is born in Warsaw, Poland

1871
Pierre Curie's father tends the wounded of the Paris Commune uprising

1877–1878
Marie begins her schooling; Pierre earns the equivalent of a master's degree in physics

1880–1881
Pierre Curie and his brother Jacques demonstrate piezoelectricity in crystals

1883
Marie graduates from a gymnasium (secondary school) for girls

1884–1885
Marie attends the floating university

1886
Marie begins to work as a governess to help support her sister Bronisława's university studies

1891
After having to give up the possibility of marrying the mathematician Casimir Zorawski, Marie joins her older sister in Paris at the Sorbonne

1893
Marie receives her undergraduate degree in physics and begins working at an industrial laboratory

1894
Continuing to study as she works, Marie earns a degree in mathematics; Marie is given her first laboratory project; Marie meets Pierre Curie

1894–1895
Marie returns briefly to Warsaw but is rejected for a post at Krakow University because she is a woman; Marie returns to Paris and joins Pierre

1895
Pierre completes his doctorate and is promoted to full professor; Marie and Pierre are married; Wilhelm Roentgen discovers X-rays

1896
Henri Becquerel discovers radioactivity in uranium; aided by the electroscope invented by Pierre and his brother, Marie investigates uranium and shows that radioactivity is an inherent property of certain atoms and does not depend on any chemical reaction

September 12, 1897
Marie and Pierre's first daughter, Irène, is born

1898
Now joined actively by Pierre, Marie Curie publishes a paper showing that thorium is radioactive as well as announcing the discovery of a new element that she names polonium; near the end of the year, the Curies announce the discovery of another new element, radium; Ernest Rutherford studies uranium radiation, identifying alpha and beta rays

March 19, 1900
Fréderic Joliot is born in Paris

1902
The French Academy of Science rejects Pierre for membership; Marie's father dies

1903
Marie receives a doctoral degree from the University of Paris; Pierre is rejected for a professorship in mineralogy; together with Henri Becquerel, Marie and Pierre Curie are awarded the Nobel Prize in physics

December 6, 1904
The Curies' second daughter, Eve, is born

1905
Pierre gives his belated Nobel lecture; Pierre is accepted as a member by the French Academy of Science; Pierre and Marie investigate psychic phenomena

April 19, 1906
Pierre Curie is struck and killed by a horse-drawn vehicle; Marie is given Pierre's post at the University of Paris, making her their first woman professor

1907
Andrew Carnegie endows the Curie Foundation; work begins on the Radium Institute

1911
Marie attends the first Solvay Conference in physics; letters suggesting a romantic affair between Marie and Paul Langevin create a scandal in the popular press; Marie is awarded her second Nobel Prize (in chemistry). Despite this achievement, the French Academy of Sciences refuses to elect her a member

August 1914
The Radium Institute opens; World War I begins

September 1914
German forces approach Paris, Marie evacuates radium; German attack on Paris is repelled

1914–1918
During World War I, Marie pioneers in the use of mobile X-ray units to treat wounded soldiers

1919
Rutherford identifies the proton

1921
Marie tours the United States to raise money for research and production of radium

1925
A Radium Institute is completed in Warsaw with Marie's help; Irène receives her doctoral degree

1926
Frédéric Joliot and Irène Curie marry; Frédéric earns his doctorate

1929
Marie makes her last fund-raising trip to the United States

1932
James Chadwick confirms the existence of the neutron; Frédéric and Irène visit the Soviet Union

1933
Frédéric and Irène attend the Solvay Conference; their composite proton theory is refuted

January 1934
Frédéric and Irène create the first artificial radioactive isotope

July 4, 1934
Marie Curie dies from aplastic anemia, probably resulting from her extensive exposure to radiation

1935
Frédéric and Irène receive the Nobel Prize

1939
Frédéric does research on nuclear fission; World War II begins with the German invasion of Poland

1940
Germany invades and occupies France

1941
Eve Curie begins a career as a war correspondent

1944
Frédéric joins the Resistance fighters; France is liberated by the Allies

1945
Frédéric is appointed French High Commissioner for Nuclear Energy

1947
Frédéric helps design ZOE, the first French nuclear research reactor

1950

Frédéric and Irène are dismissed from the French nuclear commission because of their communist leanings

1955

Frédéric signs the Einstein-Russell peace manifesto

March 17, 1956

Irène dies of leukemia

August 14, 1958

Frédéric dies from radiation-induced liver problems

1995

In a national ceremony, the remains of Marie and Pierre are reinterred in France's Panthéon

1998

Poland holds a conference honoring the 100th anniversary of the discovery of radium and polonium

October 22, 2007

Eve Curie dies at the age of 102

2011

Celebrations are held commemorating the 100th anniversary of Marie Curie's 1911 Nobel Prize

Glossary

alpha particle   a helium nucleus (two protons and two neutrons) emitted as a form of radiation.

atom   the fundamental unit of a chemical element; made up of various subatomic particles such as protons, neutrons, and electrons.

atomic mass   the combined mass of all the protons, neutrons, and electrons in a particular isotope of an element.

atomic number   the number of protons found in a particular element. It is always the same for a given element.

atomic weight   the average mass of the atoms of an element, expressed in units based on 1/12 of the mass of the carbon-12 isotope.

beta particle   an electron released from an atom as part of radioactive decay.

cathode rays   energetic electrons emitted when a spark is discharged into a vacuum tube.

cloud chamber   an instrument used to reveal the tracks left by particles.

compound   a combination of atoms held together by chemical bonds (for example, water).

Curie point   the temperature at which a magnetic material changes its form of magnetism, becoming attracted to magnetic fields.

cyclotron   a circular particle accelerator that uses high-frequency electric current to propel charged particles, which are kept on track by magnets.

decay   in radioactivity, the breakdown of an atom, accompanied by the release of radiation.

electromagnetism   the interrelated action of electric current and magnetism, where each can cause the other.

electron   a negatively charged particle found in the outer parts of atoms or flowing as electric current.

electrometer   an instrument that can detect electrical charge and measure its intensity.

element   a basic substance (such as bismuth) that cannot be chemically broken down into simpler substances.

fission   the splitting of an atom that has been struck by a neutron.

fluoresce   to glow in response to absorbing light or another form of electromagnetic radiation.

gamma rays   an energetic, penetrating form of radiation.

Geiger counter   an instrument commonly used to detect and measure radioactivity.

half-life   the time it takes for half of the atoms of a radioactive substance to break down into another substance.

ionization   the process by which atoms become either negatively charged (by gaining electrons) or positively charged (by having them stripped away).

isotope   a variant form of an element that has the same atomic number but a different atomic weight.

molecule   a combination of atoms held together by chemical bonds.

neutron   a nuclear particle about the size of the proton, but without an electrical charge.

particle accelerator   a device that propels particles such as protons or ions, by means of electrical discharges and/or magnets. The resulting particles can have very high energies..

periodic table   an arrangement of the atomic elements in columns. Atomic numbers increase from left to right; elements in the same column have similar chemical properties.

piezoelectric effect   the generating of electric current by compression of certain crystals, which in turn can be compressed by applying current.

pitchblende   a variety of uranite, a dull-colored, fine-grained ore that contains small amounts of uranium.

polonium   a radioactive element discovered by Marie and Pierre Curie. It breaks down quickly and is hard to isolate.

proton   a positively charged particle found in the nucleus of the atom.

radiation therapy (or radiotherapy)   the use of radiation to treat certain conditions, particularly tumors.

radioactivity   particles or energy sent out from atoms that spontaneously break down.

radioisotope   an isotope (variant) of an element that is radioactive.

radiology   the branch of medicine that uses radiation for diagnostic imaging or therapy.

radiometric dating   the use of the known decay rate of various elements to estimate the age of geological, biological, or archaeological specimens.

radium   a highly radioactive element discovered by Marie and Pierre Curie. It is found in small amounts in certain uranium ores.

radon   a radioactive gas produced by the decay of radium.

spectroscope   (or spectrometer) an instrument that is used to observe the spectrum (pattern of lines or bands) emitted when a substance is heated. Each element has a characteristic pattern.

uranium   a heavy element (atomic number 92) that occurs naturally in a variety of compounds and is radioactive.

X-rays   a form of electromagnetic radiation that is shorter in wavelength than visible light and capable of penetrating matter.

Further Resources

Books

Brian, Denis. *The Curies: A Biography of the Most Controversial Family in Science.* Hoboken, N.J.: Wiley, 2005.

    An extensive modern biography of the Curie family, with important accounts of the activities of the Joliot-Curies during and after World War II.

Byers, Nina, and Gary Williams. *Out of the Shadows: Contributions of Twentieth-Century Women to Physics.* New York: Cambridge University Press, 2006.

    A useful collection for obtaining a broader picture of what women have achieved in science and the obstacles they continue to face.

Close, Frank. *Particle Physics: A Very Short Introduction.* New York: Oxford University Press, 2004.

    A lively introduction that will explain more about the various particles the early nuclear physicists encountered, and then survey the rather bewildering array of today's subatomic denizens.

Curie, Eve. *Marie Curie: A Biography.* New York: DaCapo Press, 2001.

    An accessible biography based on family records and correspondence, written by Marie Curie's youngest daughter. However later critics suggested that it neglected more problematic topics such as the Curie-Langevin affair.

Curie, Marie. *Pierre Curie with the Autobiographical Notes of Marie Curie.* Translated by Charlotte and Vernon Kellogg. New York: Dover Publications, 1963.

    Besides containing important material about Pierre Curie, the "notes" are the closest thing to an autobiography of Marie Curie.

Des Jardins, Julie. *The Madame Curie Complex: The Hidden History of Women in Science.* New York: Feminist Press at CUNY, 2010.

    A modern feminist account that seeks to look beyond the conventional explanations for the rarity of first-rate women scientists in the 20th century.

Analyzes the impact of a male-dominated scientific culture on the work of woman scientists.

Goldsmith, Barbara. *Obsessive Genius: The Inner World of Marie Curie.* New York: W. W. Norton, 2005.
Another modern biography that attempts to look more closely at Marie Curie's personality and the driving forces in her life.

Hellbron, J. F. *Ernest Rutherford and the Explosion of Atoms.* New York: Oxford University Press, 2003.
An accessible biography and assessment of the work of Rutherford, the pioneer physicist whose work created much of the basis of nuclear physics and was closely connected to the efforts of the Curies.

Pasachoff, Naomi. *Marie Curie and the Science of Radioactivity.* New York: Oxford University Press, 1996.
A biography with good background material explaining the science behind the Curies' work.

Plfaum, Rosalyn. *Grand Obsession: Madame Curie and Her World.* New York: Dell Doubleday, 1989.
A well-illustrated biography that focuses on the development of Marie Curie's personality and her relationships with family and husband.

Quinn, Susan. *Marie Curie: A Life.* New York: Da Capo Press, 1996.
A good biography with a scientific focus, drawing upon newly available letters between the Curies.

Redniss, Lauren. *Radioactive: Marie & Pierre Curie: A Tale of Love and Fallout.* New York: It Books, 2010.
A visually intriguing multimedia book that reads like a graphic novel. Provides an interesting contrast to the traditional biography.

Veltman, Martinus. *Facts and Mysteries in Elementary Particle Physics.* River Edge, N.J.: World Scientific Pub. Co., 2003.
Historical background, interesting stories, and unresolved scientific questions about the many particles that have been discovered since the late 19th century.

Internet Resources

About.com. "Nuclear Power: Timeline of Nuclear Technology and the Atomic Bomb." Available online. URL: http://inventors.about.com/od/timelines/tp/nuclear.htm. Accessed May 18, 2011.
A good time line with links, to the mid-1950s.

Access to Excellence Reference Collection. "Radioactive Materials." Available online. URL: http://www.accessexcellence.org/AE/AEC/CC/radio_table. php. Accessed May 16, 2011.

A list of radioactive elements and isotopes, briefly describing common uses for each substance.

American Institute of Physics. "Women in Physics." Available online. URL: http://www.aip.org/statistics/trends/gendertrends.html. Accessed May 16, 2011.

Provides employment statistics, resources, and news relating to women in physics.

"A Brief History of Poland: Part 9: The 19th Century—Polish Wars and Uprisings." Polonia Today. Available online. URL: http://www.poloniatoday. com/history9.htm. Accessed May 16, 2011.

Summary of Polish history in the 19th century, with illustrations. Provides good background for the early years of the Skłodowska family.

Center for History of Physics, American Institute of Physics. Available online. URL: http://www.aip.org/history/. Accessed May 16, 2011.

Provides a collection of resources and conducts educational programs.

Froman, Nanny. "Marie and Pierre Curie and the Discovery of Polonium and Radium." Nobelprize.org. Available online. URL: http://nobelprize.org/ nobel_prizes/physics/articles/curie/. Accessed May 16, 2011.

Biographies from the official Nobel Prize Web site.

History Learning Site. "The French Resistance." Available online. URL: http:// www.historylearningsite.co.uk/french_resistance.htm. Accessed May 16, 2011.

Background on the development of the French Resistance in World War II in which Frédéric Joliot-Curie played a significant part. Describes their actions against the German occupation.

Maria Skłodowska-Curie, 1867–1934. Available online. URL: http://www. staff.amu.edu.pl/~zbzw/ph/sci/msc.htm. Accessed May 16, 2011.

Contains a biography including numerous Web links.

Marie Curie and the Science of Radioactivity. American Institute of Physics. Available online. URL: http://www.aip.org/history/curie/. Accessed May 16, 2011.

An online exhibit with a variety of biographical details, largely based on the book Marie Curie and the Science of Radioactivity *by Naomi Paschoff.*

"Nuclear History Timeline." Online Education.net Available online. URL: http://www.onlineeducation.net/resources/nuclear-history-timeline. Accessed May 16, 2011.

Details of events relating to nuclear weapons, power, and the cold war— mainly starting in the 1940s.

"Radiation Therapy for Cancer." National Cancer Institute. Available online. URL: http://www.cancer.gov/cancertopics/factsheet/Therapy/radiation. Accessed May 16, 2011.

An overview of the different types of radiotherapy and how they are used today to treat cancer.

University of Colorado at Boulder. "Build an Atom." Available online. URL: http://phet.colorado.edu/en/simulation/build-an-atom. Accessed May 16, 2011.

An interactive simulation allowing the user to construct an atom from protons, neutrons, and electrons, observing changes in the net charge, mass, and element represented.

Index